THE COLLECTOR'S GUIDE TO
SHAWNEE POTTERY

By Duane and Janice Vanderbilt

COLLECTOR BOOKS
A Division of Schroeder Publishing Co., Inc.

The current values in this book should be used only as a guide. They are not intended to set prices, which vary from one section of the country to another. Auction prices as well as dealer prices vary greatly and are affected by condition as well as demand. Neither the Authors nor the Publisher assumes responsibility for any losses that might be incurred as a result of consulting this guide.

Searching For A Publisher?

We are always looking for knowledgeable people considered to be experts within their fields. If you feel that there is a real need for a book on your collectible subject and have a large comprehensive collection, contact us.

COLLECTOR BOOKS
P.O. Box 3009
Paducah, Kentucky 42002-3009

Cover Design by Duane Vanderbilt and Robert Smith

Cover Layout: Beth Summers
Book Design: Gail Ashburn

Acknowledgments

We would like to thank the following people for taking the time to supply us with information for this book.

Bob Adams	Mary Louise Steil
Ruth Axline	Martha Rose Thomas
Louise Bauer	Bernard Twiggs
John F. Bonistall	George Williams
Greg & Mary Ann Garrett	Floyd Wetzel
Robert Heckman	The Ohio Historical Society
Norris Schneider	Jess Parentice
Edith Dozer	Jim & Bev Mangus

We would also like to thank the following people for supplying us with pieces or pictures of Shawnee.

Louise Bauer	Fred & Denise (Dakoulis) Strunk
Terry & Sandy Bauer	Robert & Chris Smith
Pam Curran	Ron & Debbie Smith
Dan Graber	Jim & Betty Twiggs
Ted Hansen	Bernard Twiggs
Steve & Shirley Hass	Chic & Betty Willey
Cecil & Mary Rapp	Juan Klinehoffer

We would also like to offer a special thanks to:

Robert Smith, who helped us with the design of the front cover.

Greg & Mary Ann Garrett, who let me stay with them while I was in Zanesville.

Paul & Joy Schneider, for letting us take over their house for two days, while we were taking pictures of their collection.

Bob & Candy Pemberton, for telling us we should do a book on Shawnee.

Bernard Twiggs & Robert Heckman, for patiently answering so many questions for us.

And to Louise Bauer, who has become a very special friend. Her contributions to the pottery industry are second to none.

Preface

This book will examine the history of the Shawnee Pottery Company and the items they produced. We have concentrated on the kitchenware pieces only: Cookie Jars, Salt and Peppers, Creamers, Pitchers, Teapots, and Cornware. We did not intend to offend those who collect planters, vases, and other items, but there are so many of them, we did not have time for the research involved. We hope that in the future we will be able to write a book featuring items not included in this publication.

Pricing

Prices in this book, at the time of writing, reflect current market values as close as can be estimated with information gathered from various collectors and dealers, coast to coast. Some may feel the prices are too high, others too low. What we tried to reflect in the prices is the average price per piece in consideration of regional economic differences.

Table of Contents

A Brief History of Shawnee Pottery

In 1937, the former plant of the American Encaustic Tiling Company was acquired by Malcolm A. Schweiker and his brother Roy W. Schweiker as the major shareholders of the Franklin Tile Company. The plant was laid out on the basis of a two-fire process, which was considered an expensive process for tile manufacturing. It was decided that the two-fire process would be ideal for the manufacture of decorated pottery. Addis E. Hull, Jr., a ceramic engineer, and at that time the president and general manager of the family owned A.E. Hull Pottery Company of Crooksville, was hired as president of the newly formed company. Robert C. Shilling who had been with the American Encaustic Tiling Company was hired as vice-president and for several years was in complete charge of manufacturing operations. Other key personnel were hired, George Schweber (in charge of modeling the pottery pieces), Clifford & Bernard Twiggs, and Louise Bauer (in-house designer).

Louise Bauer

From an arrowhead found in her backyard, Louise designed an arrowhead with the profile of a Shawnee Indian Head. This was chosen as the company's official trademark. This official trademark was used on the cover of the annual reports throughout the company's history. The trademark can also be found on a few of the first pieces produced and on some advertising and promotional items.

Production officially began in August of 1937. The first lines produced were in-house designs presented to and purchased by the buyers of such companies as S.S. Kresge Company, F.W. Woolworth company, and the McCrory Stores Corporation. Within a few months after Shawnee

Arrowhead

began production, Sears Roebuck and Company commissioned them to design and produce a dinnerware and kitchenware line. A bright colored dinnerware was designed and was named Valencia.

Early in 1938 the Rum Rill Pottery Company moved production from the Red Wing Pottery Company of Minnesota to Shawnee. Rum Rill was an art pottery that competed with both the Weller and Roseville lines. Designs came from both their designers and Miss Bauer. Also in 1938, Rudy Ganz, a pottery designer, was hired and Louise Bauer left Shawnee to freelance and later to join the Hull Pottery Company. Mr. Addis E. Hull, Jr. noted in a letter to Norris F. Schneider in 1960, that the principal products produced from 1937 to 1942 were decorative vases, flower pots, dishes, and figurines for various five and dimes and chain stores. During this period the two-fire process was used first to fire the clay pieces and then the china underglaze was applied and the item would be fired once again. Paint on the cookie jars and decorated bases and planters was then applied. This is what is referred to as cold paint, as the piece was not glazed and fired again. Items produced during this time were void of decorations and carried only a "U.S.A." mark on the bottom.

From October of 1942 until July of 1946, 90% of the factory was turned over to the Army-Air Force for the production of war contracts. In 1945, Robert Heckman joined Shawnee as a

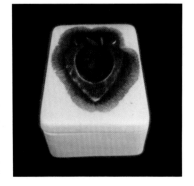

Official trademark

designer. Mr. Heckman designed such items as: the King Corn line, the Pennsylvania Dutch line, the small figurines, numerous salt & pepper sets, and many planters and vases. Shawnee officials, designers, and a small production staff remained busy during the war. They worked on designs of kitchen items that would be marketed as their own line. They applied for patents on these designs and other previously produced in-house designs. A small wartime manufacturing unit was constructed and was used for developing and testing more modern methods of producing pottery. To produce a satisfactory dollar volume in such a small manufacturing plant, they found it advisable to manufacture highly decorated, more expensive articles. At this time paint under glaze and the embossed designs were introduced. Many of the figural items and the King Corn dinnerware line sought by Shawnee collectors were designed and patented during this period.

Due to the slowed economy during the war, Shawnee and the other potteries found their customers heavily curtailing their buying in 1947 because of their large carry-over of pottery stocks. Even though new designs were provided to the wholesale jobbers, another outlet for sales had to be found to purchase the seconds and overruns. These potteries were usually built in someone's garage and only had one kiln. These small potteries would take the pieces purchased from the large potteries and add decals and gold paint, then fire the pieces again at a lower temperature. Shaffers, one of these such potteries dealt in large volume with Shawnee and was said by a neighbor to haul the pieces in by the carload. The combination of the hand decorating by Shawnee and the additional decoration by these small potteries make the pieces produced during these years (1944 to 1954) the most prized collector pieces. Cost cutting measures taken during this time included the introduction of Ram Presses to produce the King Corn dinnerware line. Bernard Twiggs was very instrumental in the installation of these presses.

Addis E. Hull, Jr. resigned his presidency position in 1950 to join the Western Stoneware Company in Monmouth, Illinois and was replaced by Albert P. Braid. The new decade also brought about changes in the American economy. The "Buy American" campaigns had been left in the previous decade and foreign competition was beginning to reach pre-war levels. With the combination of higher post-war wages and foreign competition, profit levels were shrinking. The year of 1953 resulted in a record loss.

A new president, Mr. John F. Bonistall, was elected by the board of directors in 1954 in hopes of a turnabout in company profits. Mr. Bonistall's plans to increase profits included changes in both the manufacturing and designs of the pottery produced by the company. His first plan of action was to cut manufacturing costs. He did this by eliminating the hand painting process and introducing a spray painting process which drastically cut the man hours required per piece. The spray painting process went hand and hand with the change in designs. Mr. Bonistall changed the emphasis from kitchenware items to decorative items. The items produced during this period, from 1954 to the closing of the company in 1961, can be divided into three categories. A separate division, Kenwood Ceramics, was created to produce a more modern style of kitchenware items. The King Corn dinnerware line was phased out and replaced with the more modern colored Queen Corn line. The third category consists of the numerous art pottery lines that produced decorative vases, planters, and bathroom tile. These sophisticated lines were given descriptive names and were marketed under the Shawnee name.

The Shawnee Pottery Company ceased operations in 1961 after many successful years. The molds for the figural cookie jars (Muggsy, Winnie, Smiley) of the postwar period were sold to a company know as Terrace Ceramics. Terrace produced the cookie jars void of color or decoration.

Unique Facts About Shawnee Production

❖ Casting molds did not have straps or clamps and each mold was made in four pieces.

❖ Molds were filled 2, 3, or 4 at a time depending on the number across the table.

❖ Plaster for the casting molds was mixed under a vacuum with nothing less than 100 lbs. mixed at a time.

❖ Bisque kiln (drying oven) was elevated with loading of cars under the kiln.

❖ Casting machines were designed so molds could be dried fast. This was copied by many other potteries. The Ferris wheel type machine became quite popular.

❖ Casting slip was heated.

❖ All items were packaged in air cell cartons so no packing material was needed.

❖ Workers were time studied and a bonus system was used.

❖ Shawnee would sometimes purchase items produced by Japanese companies and copy them.

Design and Production Dates of Selected Items

Sunflower-Original Shapes...Prior to 1945
Elephant Teapots without Lids 1945
Sailor Boy Cookie Jar ....(not produced after 1945)
Bull Dog & Tumbling Bear Banks...1945-1946
Small Figurines 1945-1946
Embossed Cloverbud Items 1945-1946
Duck Shakers 1946
Elephant Teapots Lids Added...1946
Chef S&P 1946-1947
Swiss Children Shakers 1947-1948
Embossed Sunflower 1947-1948
Little Chef Cookie Jar 1947-1948
Drum Major Cookie Jar..1947-1948
Pennsylvania Dutch...1949-1950
Water Bucket Sugar Bowl/Utility Jar 1949-1950
Howdy Doody Bank (only produced one year) 1950-1951
Pie Bird & Sock Darner...1951-1952

Labels

The following are labels that can be found on Shawnee Pottery.

Palette & Brush – found on gold trimmed Cookie Jars

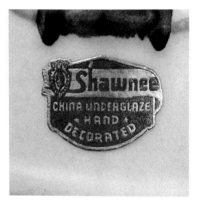

Shawnee china under glaze hand decorated

Shawnee Sample Label – these labels were applied on pieces that were taken to pottery shows

Essex China Label

Labels not pictured: Corn King ovenproof, Darn-Aid found on the sock darners.

Kenwood Zanesville Ohio – applied to the Kenwood Lines, such as Lobster Ware, the pink Elephant, and possibly the Sundial pieces

LeMieux China – this is a gold ring stamp found on pieces that are gold trimmed or gilt entirely in gold

Cookie Jars

**Plate 1. Smiley
Marked USA**

**Plate 2. Smiley – Red Cold Paint
Marked USA**

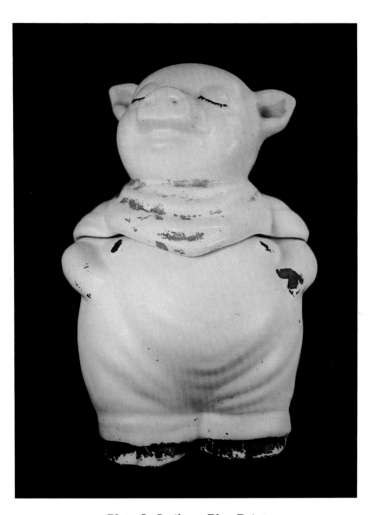

**Plate 3. Smiley – Blue Paint
Marked USA**

These Smileys above are cold painted or plain. The tops and bottoms of these will not interchange with the tops and bottoms of the paint under the glaze Smileys. The rim is more triangular on the plain and cold paint Smileys as opposed to a round opening on the under the glaze ones.

Plate 4. Smiley – Blue Bib
Marked USA

Plate 5. Smiley – Clover Bud
Marked Pat. Smiley USA

The Smiley with Clover Buds in Plate 5 is the only Smiley that is patented. To find this jar with gold trim would be a rare find.

Plate 6. Smiley – Tulips
Marked USA

Plate 7. Smiley – Chrysanthemums
Marked USA

**Plate 8. Smiley – Shamrocks
Marked USA**

**Plate 9. Smiley Bank
Chocolate Bottom
Marked Shawnee Smiley 60**

**Plate 10. Smiley Bank
Butterscotch Bottom
Marked Shawnee Smiley 60**

**Plate 11. Smiley
Butterscotch Bottom
Marked Shawnee Smiley 60**

This is not a bank. It is the same size as the bank head jars, but there is no slot in the head, and the bottom of the head is open.

Plate 12. Smiley – Plums
Marked USA

Plate 14. Smiley – Apples
Marked USA

There is an interesting story behind this Smiley in Plate 14. It was given to Louis Bauer while she was at Hull Pottery. She used this Smiley to model the head of the Red Riding Hood cookie jar. She told us, the way the head of the Smiley was designed was so unique she wanted to use it for the Red Riding Hood.

Plate 13. Smiley – Apples
Marked USA

**Plate 15. Smiley Bank With Gold
Chocolate Bottom
Marked Shawnee Smiley 60**

**Plate 16. Smiley – Strawberries
Gold Trim
Marked USA**

**Plate 17. Smiley – Gold With Decals
Marked USA**

**Plate 18a. Smiley – Gold With Decals
Marked USA**

**Plate 18b. Smiley – Gold & Decals
Toupee Painted On Head
Marked USA**

**Plate 18c. Smiley – Gold & Decals
Flies Painted On Head
Marked USA**

**Plate 18d. Smiley Shamrocks & Gold
Butterfly On Head
Marked USA**

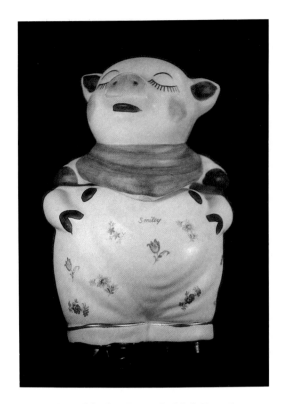

Plate 20. Smiley – Gold & Decals
Marked USA

Plate 19. Smiley – Gold & Decals
Marked USA

Plate 21. Smiley – Gold & Decals
Marked USA

Plate 22. Smiley - Gold & Decals
Marked USA

Plate 23. Smiley – Shamrocks With Gold
Marked USA

Plate 24. Smiley – Tulips & Gold
Marked USA

Plate 25. Smiley – Chrysanthemums
Gold Trim
Marked USA

Plate 26. Winnie – Peach Collar
Marked Pat. Winnie USA

Plate 27. Winnie – Blue Collar
Marked USA

Plate 28. Winnie – Green Collar
Marked USA

Plate 29. Winnie – Clover Bud
Marked Pat. Winnie USA

Plate 30. Winnie Bank
Butterscotch Bottom
Marked Shawnee Winnie 61

**Plate 31. Winnie Bank
Chocolate Bottom
Marked Shawnee Winnie 61**

**Plate 32. Winnie – Apples & Gold
Marked USA**

**Plate 33. Winnie – Clover Bud
Gold Trim
Marked Pat. Winnie USA**

**Plate 34. Winnie – Blue Collar
Gold Trim
Marked USA**

**Plate 35. Winnie – Red Collar
Gold Trim
Marked USA**

Plate 35 & 36 Winnies have red collars. The red has been applied over a green, blue or peach collar. It is not cold paint, it is fired-on enamel. They did not produce a red collar Winnie like the Smileys.

**Plate 36. Winnie – Red collar
Gold Trim
Marked USA**

**Plate 37. Winnie – Peach Collar
Gold Trim
Marked Pat. Winnie USA**

**Plate 38. Winnie Bank
Chocolate Bottom With Gold
Marked Shawnee Winnie 61**

**Plate 39. Muggsy
Marked USA**

**Plate 40. Muggsy – Gold Trim
No Decals
Marked Pat. Muggsy USA**

**Plate 41. Muggsy – Gold With Decals
Marked Pat. Muggsy USA**

Plate 42. Muggsy – Gold With Decals
Marked Pat. Muggsy USA

Plate 43a. Muggsy Gold With Decals
Marked Pat. Muggsy USA

Plate 43b. Muggsy – Green Scarf
Gold Trim & Decals
Marked Pat. Muggsy USA

Plate 44. Puss'n Boots
Marked Pat. Puss'n Boots

Plate 45. Puss'n Boots
Tail Over Foot
Marked Pat. Puss'n Boots

Plate 46. Puss'n Boots
Gold Trim & Decals
Marked Pat. Puss'n Boots

**Plate 47. Puss'n Boots
Gold Trim & Decals
Marked Pat. Puss'n Boots**

**Plate 48. Puss'n Boots
Gold & Decals
Marked Pat. Puss'n Boots**

**Plate 49. Puss'n Boots
Tail Over Foot
Gold With Decals
Marked Pat. Puss'n Boots**

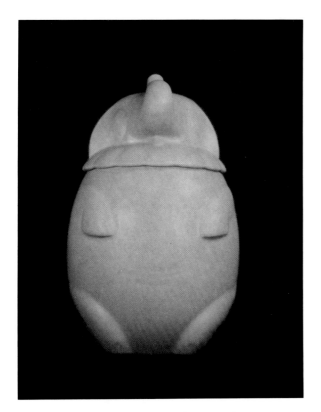

**Plate 50. Pink Elephant
Marked Shawnee 60**

Originally designed as an ice server.

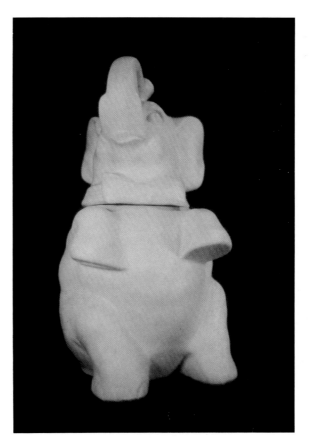

**Plate 51. Sitting Elephant
Marked USA**

**Plate 52. Sitting Elephant
Cold Paint
Marked USA**

**Plate 53a. Sitting Elephant
Gold Trim & Decals
Marked USA**

There is also an Elephant with a red over green collar.

**Plate 53b. Sitting Elephant
With Fly On Tusk
Gold & Decals
Marked USA**

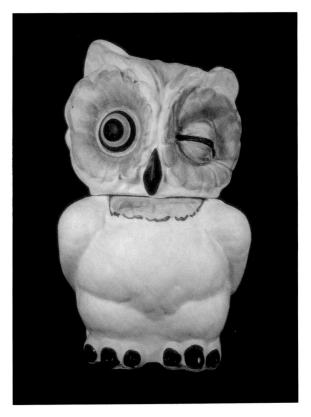

Plate 54. Owl
Marked USA

Plate 55. Owl – Gold Trim
Marked USA

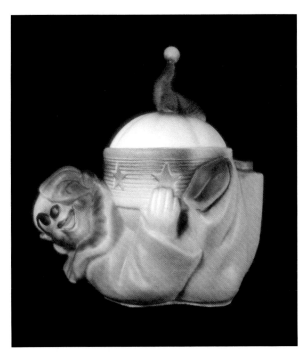

Plate 56. Jo Jo the Clown
Marked Shawnee 12

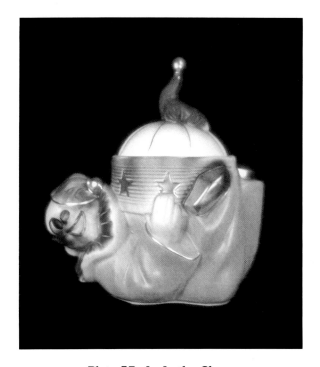

Plate 57. Jo Jo the Clown
Gold Trim
Marked Shawnee 12

Plate 58. Drum Major
Marked USA 10

Plate 59. Drum Major
Gold Trim
Marked USA 10

Plate 60. Little Chef – White
Marked USA

The Chef jar in Plate 60 is also available in yellow and blue.

Plate 61. Little Chef – Cream Color
Marked USA

Plate 62. Little Chef – Green
Marked USA

Plate 63. Little Chef – Brown/Cold Paint
Marked USA

Plate 64. Little Chef – White With Gold Trim
Marked USA

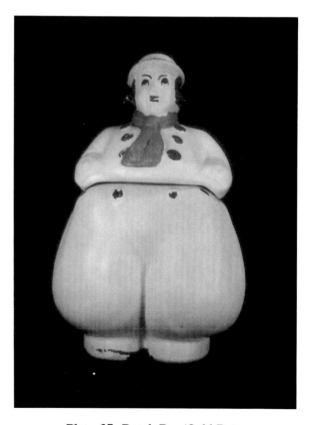

Plate 65. Dutch Boy/Cold Paint
Marked USA

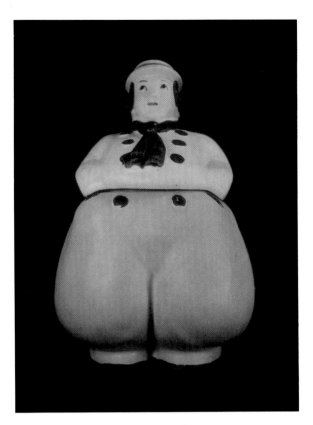

Plate 66. Dutch Boy
Marked USA

Plate 67. Dutch Boy – With Stripes
Marked USA

Plate 68. Dutch Boy
Double Stripes
Marked USA

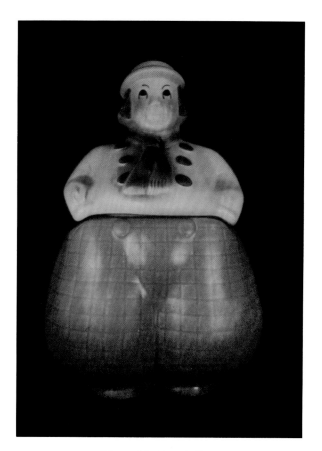

Plate 69. Dutch Boy
Great Northern
Marked Great Northern 1025

Plate 70. Dutch Boy With Stripes
Gold & Decals
Marked USA

Plate 71. Dutch Boy With Stripes
Gold & Decals
Marked USA

Plate 72. Dutch Boy
Gold & Decals
Marked USA

Plate 73. Dutch Boy
Gold Trim & Decals
Marked USA

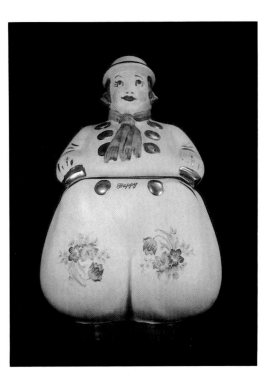

Plate 74. Dutch Boy
Gold & Decals
Marked USA

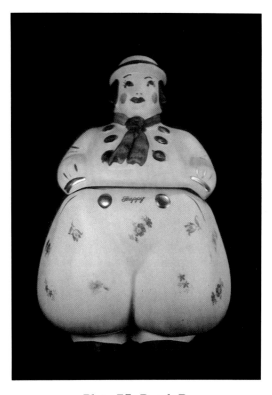

Plate 75. Dutch Boy
Gold & Decals
Marked USA

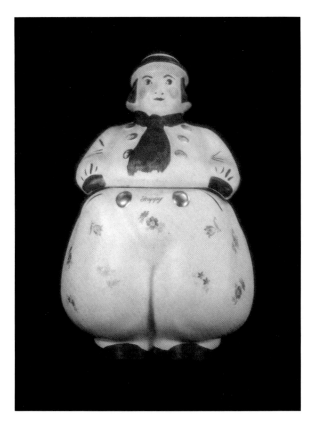

Plate 76. Dutch Boy
Gold & Decals
Marked USA

Plate 77. Dutch Boy
Gold & Decals
Marked USA

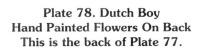
Plate 78. Dutch Boy
Hand Painted Flowers On Back
This is the back of Plate 77.

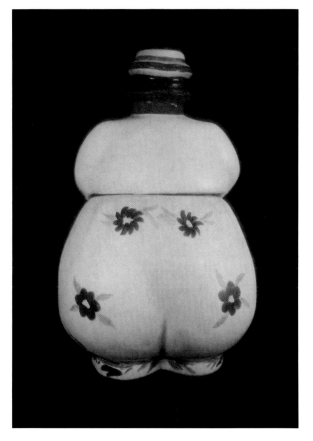

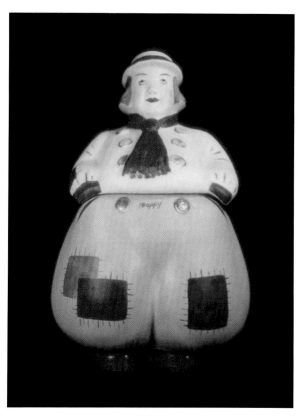

Plate 79. Dutch Boy – Patches
Gold Trim
Marked USA

Plate 80. Dutch Boy – Patches
Gold Trim
Marked USA

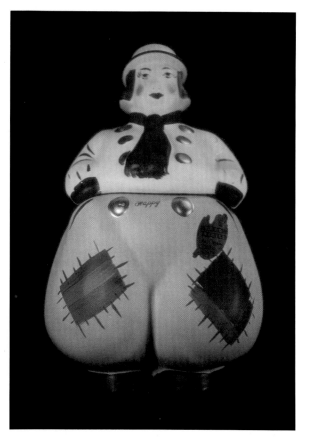

Plate 81. Dutch Boy – Patches
Gold Trim
Marked USA

Plate 82. Dutch Girl – Cold Paint
Marked USA

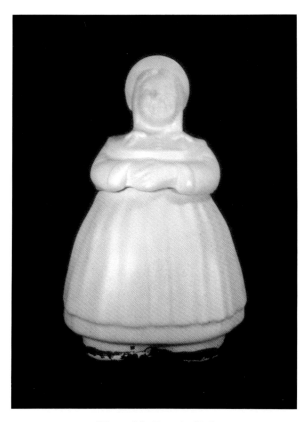

Plate 83. Dutch Girl
Marked USA

Plate 84. Dutch Girl
Paint Under Glaze
Marked USA

Plate 85. Dutch Girl
Paint Under Glaze
Marked USA

Plate 87. Great Northern Dutch Girl
Marked Great Northern 1026

Plate 86. Dutch Girl – Tulip
Marked USA

Plate 88. Dutch Girl – Great Northern
Marked Great Northern 1026

**Plate 89. Dutch Girl – Gold decals
Marked USA**

**Plate 90. Dutch Girl – Gold Decals
Marked USA**

**Plate 91. Dutch Girl
Gold Trim & Decals
Marked USA**

**Plate 92. Dutch Girl
Gold Trim & Decals**

**Plate 94. Dutch Girl
Gold Trim & Decals
Marked USA**

**Plate 93. Dutch Girl
Gold Trim & Decals
Marked USA**

**Plate 95. Dutch Girl
Gold Trim & Decals
Marked USA**

Plate 96. Dutch Girl
Gold Trim & Decals
Marked USA

Plate 97. Dutch Girl – Tulips
Gold Trim & Decals
Marked USA

Plate 98. Dutch Girl – Tulip
Gold Trim & Decals
Marked USA

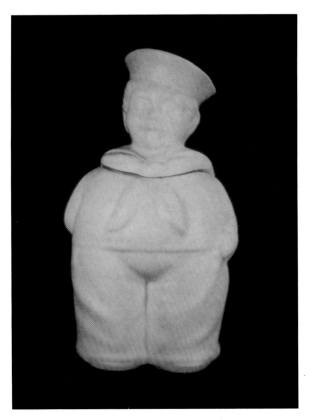

Plate 99. Sailor Boy
Marked USA

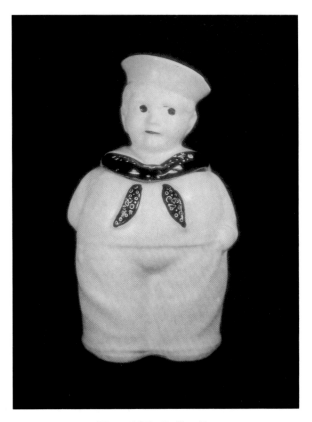

Plate 100. Sailor Boy
Marked USA

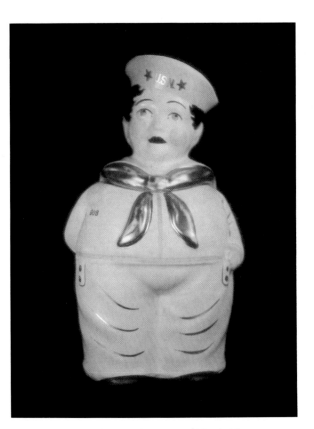

Plate 101. Sailor Boy – Black Hair
Gold Trim
Marked USA

Plate 102. Sailor Boy – Blonde Hair
Gold Trim
Marked USA

Plate 104. Fruit Basket
Marked Shawnee 84

Plate 103. Sailor Boy
Gold & Decals
Marked USA

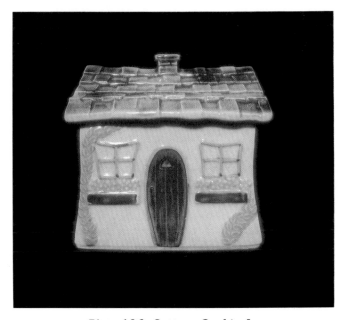

Plate 105. Fruit Basket
Gold Trim
Marked Shawnee 84

Plate 106. Cottage Cookie Jar
Marked USA 6

**Plate 107. Blue Jug With Paint
Over The Glaze Flowers
Marked USA**

**Plate 108. Blue Jug
Marked USA**

**Plate 109. Yellow Jug
Marked USA
Also With Painted Flowers Like Plate 107**

**Plate 110. Green Jug
Marked USA**

**Plate 111. Pennsylvania Dutch
Marked USA**

**Plate 112. Hexagon – Basketweave
Marked USA**

**Plate 113. Hexagon – Basketweave
Marked USA**

**Plate 114. Hexagon – Basketweave
Gold Trim & Decals
Marked USA**

Plate 115. Hexagon Basketweave
Gold Trim & Decals
Marked USA

Plate 116. Hexagon Basketweave
Gold Trim & Decals
Marked USA

Plate 117. Octagon
Fernware
Marked USA

Plate 118. Octagon
Fernware
Marked USA
Slightly Larger Than Plate 117

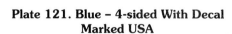

**Plate 120. Green – 4-sided
With Decal
Marked USA**

**Plate 119. Beanpot
Snowflake
Marked USA
Also In Blue & Green**

**Plate 121. Blue – 4-sided With Decal
Marked USA**

**Plate 122. Yellow – 4-sided
Hand Decorated Gold Trim
Marked USA**

**Plate 123. Yellow – 4-sided
Painted Flowers & Gold
Marked USA**

**Plate 124. Smiley
Peach Flower
Marked Pat. Smiley**

**Plate 125. Smiley
Red Flower
Marked Pat. Smiley
USA**

**Plate 126. Smiley
Clover Bud
Marked Pat. Smiley USA**

**Plate 127. Smiley
Apple
Marked Pat. Smiley USA**

There is a Smiley with the Clover Buds trimmed in gold and very rare.

This Smiley looks like the Clover Bud. It is an apple painted over the Clover Bud, under the glaze.

Plate 128. Smiley – With Gold
Red Flower
Marked Pat. Smiley

Plate 129. Smiley – With Gold
Peach Flower
Marked Pat. Smiley

Plate 130. Smiley – With Gold
Red Flower
Marked Pat. Smiley USA

Plate 131. Charlie Chicken
Marked Pat. Charlicleer

Plate 132. Charlie Chicken
Gold & Decals
Marked Charlicleer

Plate 133. Charlie Chicken
Gold & Decals
Marked Charlicleer

Plate 134. Charlie Chicken
Gold & Decals
Marked Charlicleer

Plate 135. Charlie Chicken
Gold Trim
Marked Charlicleer

Plate 136. Charlie Chicken
Gold Trim
Marked Charlicleer

Plate 138. Bo Peep
Blue Bonnet
Marked Pat. Bo Peep

Plate 137. Charlie Chicken
All Gold
Marked Charlicleer

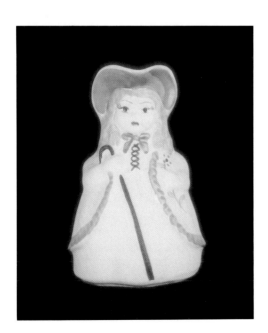

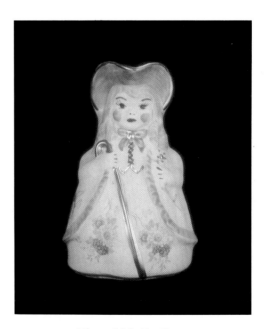

Plate 140. Bo Peep
Gold & Decals
Marked Pat. Bo Peep

Plate 139. Bo Peep
Lavender Bonnet
Marked Pat. Bo Peep

Plate 141. Bo Peep
Gold Trim No Decals
Marked Pat. Bo Peep

Plate 142. Bo Peep
Gold With Decals
Marked Pat. Bo Peep

Plate 143. Bo Peep
Gold With Decals
Marked Pat. BoPeep

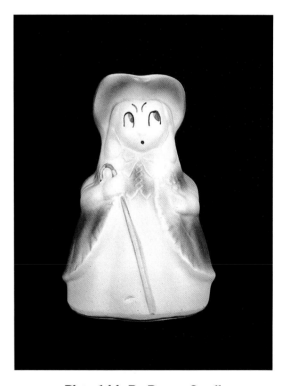

Plate 144. Bo Peep – Small
Marked Shawnee 47

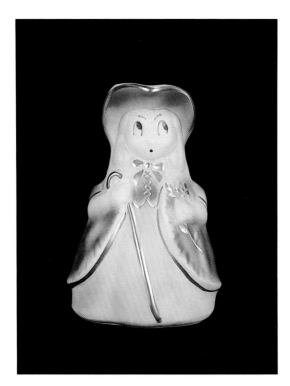

**Plate 145. Bo Peep – Small
Gold Trim
Marked Shawnee 47**

**Plate 146. Boy Blue
Marked Shawnee 46**

**Plate 147. Boy Blue
Gold Trim
Marked Shawnee 46**

**Plate 148. Pennsylvania Dutch
Marked USA 64**

**Plate 149. Sunflower
Marked USA**

**Plate 150. Tulip
Marked USA**

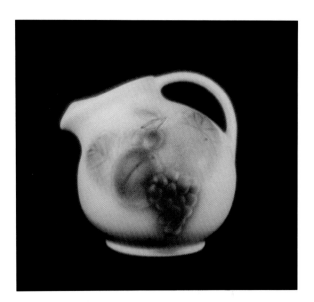

**Plate 151. Fruit
Marked Shawnee 80**

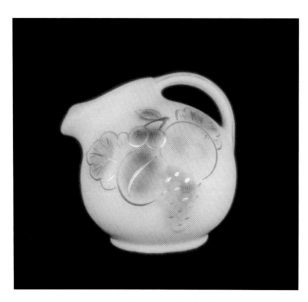

**Plate 152. Fruit With Gold
Marked Shawnee 80**

The Pennsylvania Dutch Coffeepot came in two sizes: the #52 (pictured) and the smaller #42. They also came with a percolator top made of aluminum or ceramic that are extremely hard to find.

Plate 154. Sunflower
Coffeepot
Marked USA

Plate 153. Pennsylvania Dutch
Coffeepot
Marked USA 52

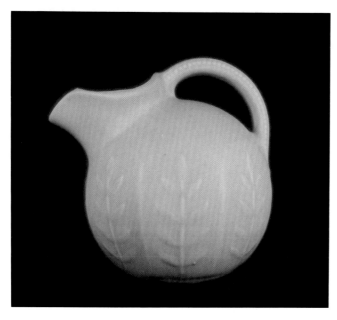

Plate 155. Octagon Jug
Fernware
Marked USA

Plate 156. Octagon Jug
Fernware
Marked USA

Plate 157. Ball Jug
Snowflake
Marked USA

Plate 158. Jug Pitcher
Flower & Fern

Creamers

**Plate 159. Smiley
Peach Flower
Marked Pat. Smiley**

**Plate 160. Smiley
Clover Bud
Marked Pat. Smiley**

**Plate 161. Smiley
Blue & Yellow
Marked Shawnee 86**

**Plate 162. Smiley With Gold
Peach Flower
Marked Pat. Smiley**

**Plate 163. Smiley – With Gold
Blue & Yellow
Marked Shawnee 86**

Plate 164 is just like Plate 163 except for the solid gold nose.

**Plate 164. Smiley – With Gold
Yellow & Blue
Marked Shawnee 86**

**Plate 165. Smiley – Clover Bud
Gold Trim
Marked Pat. Smiley**

**Plate 166. Puss'n Boots
Marked Pat.
Puss'n Boots**

Plate 167. Puss'n Boots
Cream Color
Marked Pat. Puss'n Boots

Plate 168. Puss'n Boots
Marked Pat.
Puss'n Boots

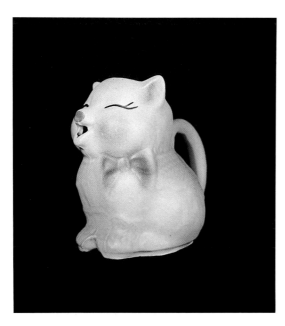

Plate 169. Puss'n Boots
Green/Yellow
Marked Shawnee 85

Plate 170. Puss'n Boots/Gold
Marked Pat.
Puss'n Boots

Plate 171. Puss'n Boots
Gold/Decals
Marked Pat. Puss'n Boots

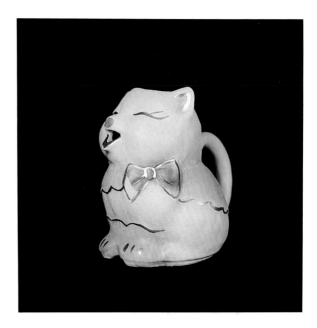

Plate 172. Puss'n Boots/Gold
Green & Yellow
Marked Shawnee 85

Plate 173. Puss'n Boots
Pink & White With Gold
Marked 85

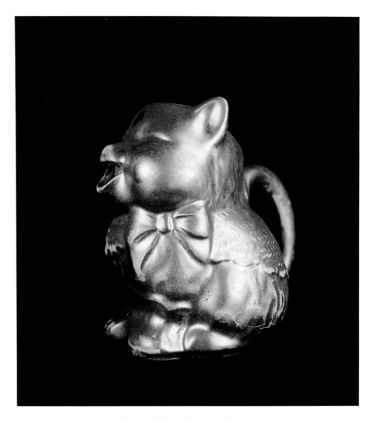

Plate 174. Puss'n Boots
All Gold
Marked Pat.
Puss'n Boots

This Puss'n Boots creamer is a factory second, the Puss'n Boots has been rubbed off, but the #85 remains.

Plate 176. Elephant
Gold Trim
Marked Pat. USA

Plate 175. Elephant
Marked Pat. USA

Plate 178. Elephant
Gold & Decals
Marked Pat. USA

Plate 177. Elephant
Gold & Decals
Marked Pat. USA

Plate 179. Elephant
Gold & Decals
Marked Pat. USA

Plate 180. Pennsylvania Dutch
Marked USA 12

Plate 181. Tulip Ball Jug
Marked USA

Plate 182. Quill Ball Jug
Marked USA 12

This ball jug creamer was made for a wartime charity in 1945.

Plate 183. Sunflower
Marked USA

Plate 184. Yellow Tilt
Marked USA 10

Also available in blue & possibly green. We have seen the blue one with painted flowers.

Plate 185. Pennsylvania Dutch
Tilt Creamer
Marked USA 10

Plate 186. Creamer With Flower
Gold Trim
Marked USA 40

Plate 187. Creamer
Flower & Fern
Marked USA

Plate 187 & Plate 188 are also available in different colors: blue, yellow, & white.

Plate 188. Creamer Snowflake
Marked USA

Large Shakers

**Plate 189. Winnie & Smiley
Heart Set**

**Plate 190. Winnie & Smiley
Clover Bud**

The Winnies in the Heart & Clover Bud sets are the only Winnies we have seen.

This set of shakers in gold are very rare.

**Plate 191. Smileys
Green Bib**

**Plate 192. Smileys
Blue Bib**

Plate 193. Smileys
Red Bib

Plate 194. Smileys – Green
Bib With Gold & Decals

Plate 195. Smileys – Green
Bib With Gold & Decals

Plate 196. Smileys – Green
Bib With Gold & Decals

**Plate 197. Smileys – Green
Bib With Gold & Decals**

**Plate 198. Smileys – Blue Bib
Gold & Decals**

**Plate 199. Smileys – Blue Bib
Gold & Decals**

**Plate 200. Smileys – Peach
Bib With Gold & Decals**

Also available plain with peach bib.

**Plate 201. Smileys – Red Bib
Gold & Decals**

**Plate 202. Smileys – Red Bib
Gold & Decals**

Plate 203. Muggsy

Plate 204. Muggsy – Gold

Plate 206. Charlie Chickens
Gold Trim

Plate 205. Charlie Chickens

Plate 208. Dutch Boy & Girl

Plate 207. Charlie Chickens
Gold Trim

The boy in this set has blue eyes, the girl has the wavy blue line on the bottom of her dress.

Plate 209. Dutch Boy & Girl

The boy in this set has brown eyes, the girl has a wide blue line on the bottom of her dress. She matches the white Great Northern cookie jar.

Plate 210. Dutch Boy & Girl
Gold & Decals

Plate 211. Dutch Boy & Girl
Gold & Decals

Plate 212. Dutch Boy & Girl
Great Northern

This is the only set we know of, very rare.

Plate 213. Dutch Boy & Girl
Gold Trim

Plate 214. Swiss Boy & Girl
Gold Trim

Plate 215. Blue Jug

Also in different colors, green & yellow.

Plate 216. Pennsylvania Dutch

Plate 217. Sunflower

Plate 218. Decorative Design

This design was originally the Pennsylvania Dutch.

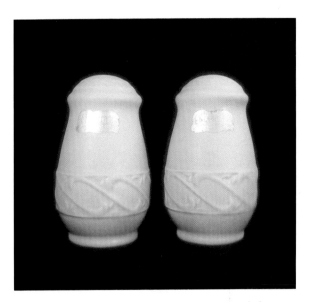

**Plate 219. Embossed Design
Blue Shakers**

**Plate 220. Embossed Design
Green Shakers**

These shakers are made to fit on the side of the fruit sugar bowl. They have hooks on the top of them.

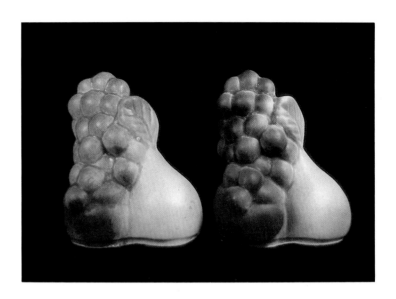

**Plate 221. Fruit Shakers
Marked USA**

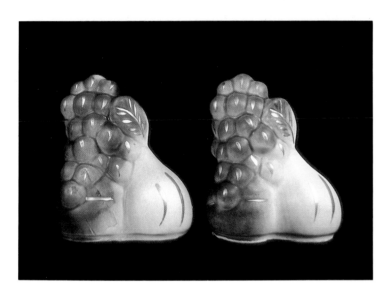

**Plate 222. Fruit Shakers
Gold Trim
Marked USA 8**

**Plate 223. Square Shakers
Flower & Fern**

This design of shaker might be available in different colors.

Small Shakers

Plate 224. Winnie & Smiley

Plate 225. Winnie & Smiley

Plate 226. Winnie & Smiley
Heart Set

**Plate 227. Winnie & Smiley
Clover Bud**

There may be a set like this with gold trim.
If so, it is very rare.

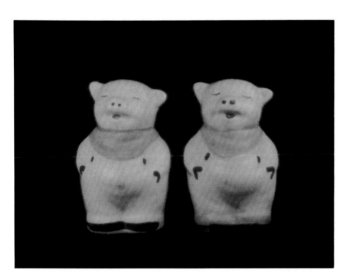

**Plate 228. Smileys
Peach Bib**

There should be small Winnies to go
with these Smileys. The small Winnies
have 3 holes & the Smileys have 4 holes.

**Plate 229. Winnie & Smiley
Gold Trim**

**Plate 230. Winnie & Smiley
Gold Trim**

**Plate 231. Smileys – Peach Bib
Gold Trim**

**Plate 232. Winnie & Smiley
Gold Trim**

Plate 234. Farmer Pigs
Gold Trim

Plate 233. Farmer Pigs

Plate 236. Puss'n Boots
Gold Trim

Plate 235. Puss'n Boots

Plate 237. Puss'n Boots
Gold trim

Plate 238. Owls – Green Eyed

They can be found with gold trim.

Plate 239. Owls

Plate 240. Owls With Gold

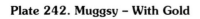

Plate 241. Muggsy

Plate 242. Muggsy – With Gold

Plate 243. Charlie Chickens

Plate 244. Charlie Chickens
Gold Trim

Plate 245. Bo Peep/Sailor Boy

**Plate 246. Bo Peep/Sailor Boy
Gold Trim**

Plate 247. Ducks

Plate 248. Milk Cans

**Plate 249. Milk Cans
Gold With Decals**

**Plate 250. Milk Cans
Gold With Decals**

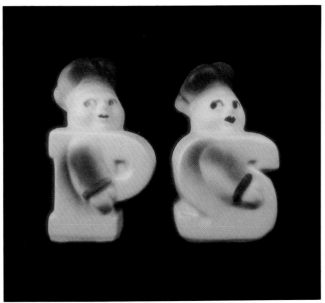

Plate 251. Chef S&P

**Plate 252. Chef S&P
Gold Trim**

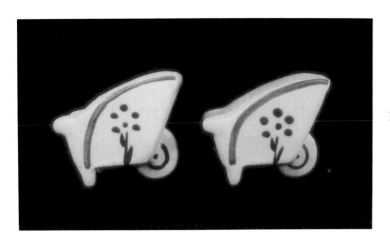

Plate 253. Wheelbarrows

**Plate 254. Wheelbarrows
Gold Trim**

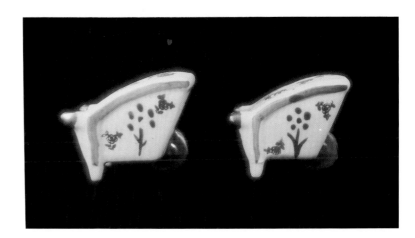

Plate 255. Watering Cans

Plate 256. Watering Cans Gold Trim

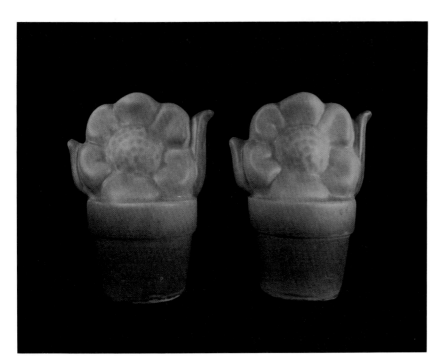

Plate 257. Flower Pots

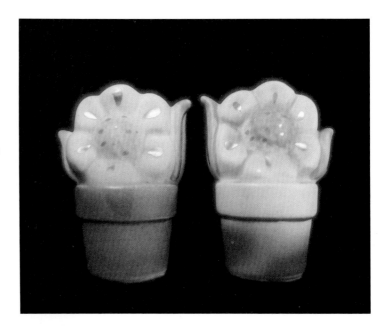

**Plate 258. Flower Pots
Gold Trim**

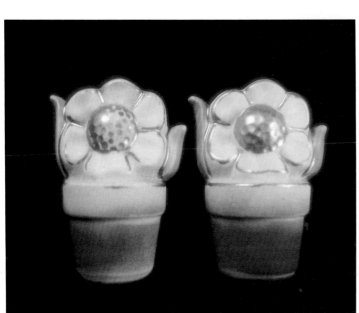

**Plate 259. Flower Pots
Gold Trim**

Plate 260. Fruit Shakers

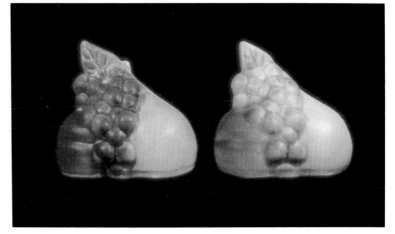

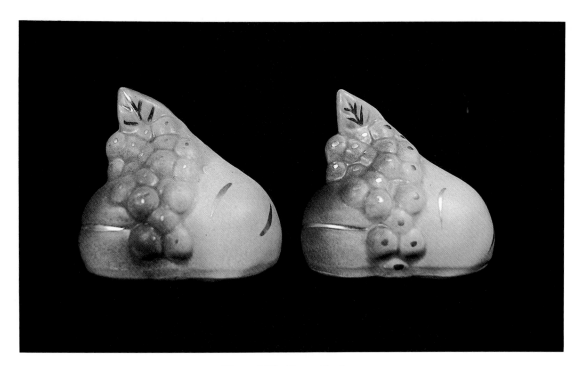

Plate 261. Fruit Shakers
Gold Trim

Plate 262. Cottage Shakers
Marked USA 9

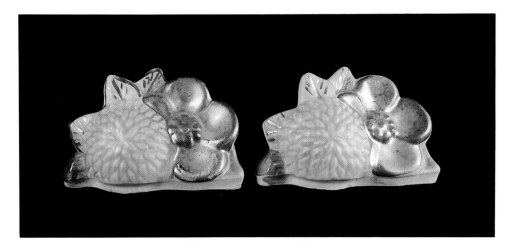

Plate 263. Flower Shakers
Gold Trim

Plate 264. Flower & Fern Shakers

Also found in different colors.

Teapots

Plate 265. Granny Ann
Green Apron
Marked Pat. Ann

Plate 266. Granny Ann
Marked Pat. Ann USA

Plate 267. Granny Ann
Marked USA

Plate 268. Granny Ann
Gold With Decals
Marked Pat. Granny Ann

Plate 269. Granny Ann
Gold With Decals
Marked USA

Plate 270. Granny Ann
Matte Finish With Gold
Marked Pat. Granny
Ann USA

Plate 271. Granny Ann
Matte Finish With Gold
Marked Pat. Granny
Ann USA

Plate 272. Tom Tom
Marked Tom The Piper's Son
Pat. USA

Plate 273. Tom Tom
Marked Tom The Piper's Son
Pat. USA

Plate 274. Tom Tom
Gold With Blue Patch
Marked Tom the Piper's Son
Pat. USA

This Tom Tom is also available with a red patch instead of a blue one.

Plate 275. Tom Tom
Gold Trim
Marked Tom the Piper's Son
Pat. USA

Plate 276. Tom Tom With Gold
Matte Finish
Marked Tom The Piper's Son
Pat. USA

Plate 277. Elephant
Marked USA

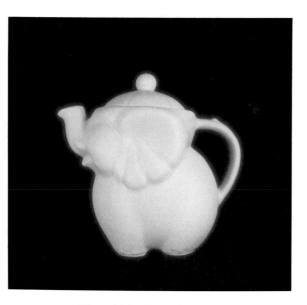

Plate 278. Blue Elephant
Marked USA

Plate 279. Green Elephant
Marked USA

Plate 280. Yellow Elephant
Marked USA

**Plate 281. Yellow Elephant
Gold Trim
Marked USA**

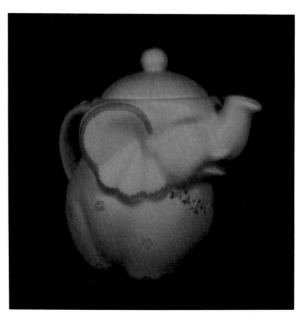

**Plate 282. Blue Elephant With Painted Flowers
Marked USA**

**Plate 283. Pennsylvania Dutch
Marked USA**

**Plate 284. Pennsylvania Dutch 27 oz.
Marked USA 27**

Plate 285. Pennsylvania Dutch 18 oz.
Marked USA 18

Plate 286. Pennsylvania Dutch 14 oz.
Marked USA 14

Plate 287. Pennsylvania Dutch 10 oz.
Marked USA 10

Plate 288. Pennsylvania Dutch 18 oz. With Gold
Marked USA 18

**Plate 289. Yellow Teapot
Marked USA 18**

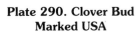

Also found in blue & breen.

**Plate 290. Clover Bud
Marked USA**

**Plate 291. Clover Bud With Gold
Marked USA**

**Plate 293. Sunflower With Gold
Marked USA**

**Plate 294. Embossed Rose
Marked USA**

**Plate 295. Embossed Rose
Gold Trim
Marked USA**

**Plate 295. Embossed Rose
Gold Trim
Marked USA**

**Plate 296. Embossed Rose
Solid Gold
Marked USA**

**Plate 297. Teapot
Blue Leaves
Marked USA**

**Plate 298. Teapot With Blue Leaves
Gold & Decals
Marked USA**

**Plate 299. Teapot
Red Flower
Marked USA**

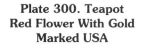

**Plate 300. Teapot
Red Flower With Gold
Marked USA**

**Plate 301. Teapot With Red & Blue Flower
Marked USA**

**Plate 302. Teapot With Blue & Red Flower
& Gold
Marked USA**

**Plate 303. Teapot – Tulip
Marked USA**

**Plate 304. Teapot – With Red Flower
Marked USA**

**Plate 305. Teapot – With Red flower
Marked USA**

**Plate 306. Teapot – With Heart-Shaped
Flower
Marked USA**

Plate 307. Teapot – With Red Flower
Marked USA

Plate 308. Teapot – With Blue Flower
Marked USA

Plate 309. Teapot – With Blue Flower & Gold
Marked USA

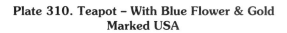
Plate 310. Teapot – With Blue Flower & Gold
Marked USA

Plate 311. Teapot – Blue
Marked USA

Plate 312. Teapot – Blue
Marked USA

**Plate 313. Teapot – Blue Embossed Design
Marked USA**

**Plate 314. Teapot – Green
Embossed Flower
Marked USA**

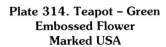

**Plate 315. Teapot – Small
Green Snowflake
Marked USA**

Like #316, this teapot comes in other colors & sizes.

**Plate 316. Teapot – Blue
Snowflake
Marked USA**

**Plate 317. Teapot – Cottage
Marked USA 7**

Miscellaneous

Plate 318. Squirrel Figurine

Plate 319. Squirrel Figurine
Gold & Decals

Plate 320. Rabbit Figurine

Plate 321. Rabbit Figurine
Gold & Decals

Plate 322. Raccoon Figurine

**Plate 323. Raccoon Figurine
Gold & Decals**

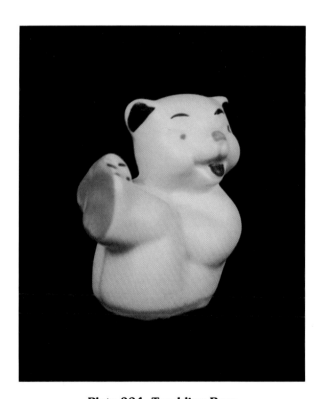

Plate 324. Tumbling Bear

**Plate 325. Tumbling Bear
Gold & Decals**

Plate 326. Tumbling Bear
Gold & Decals

Plate 327. Puppy Dog

Plate 328. Puppy Dog
Gold & Decals

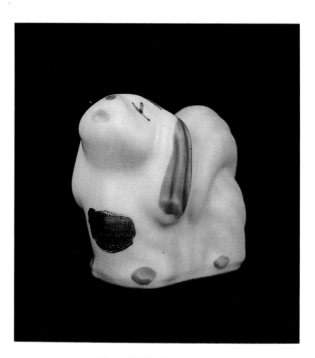

Plate 329. Pekingese

**Plate 330. Pekingese
Gold & Decals**

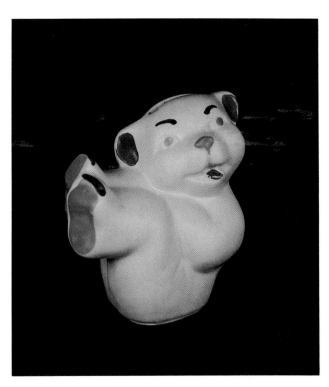

Plate 332. Tumbling Bear Bank

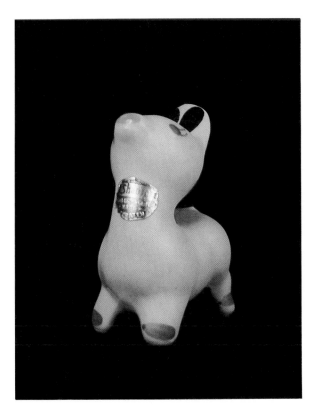

Plate 331. Deer Figurine

Plate 333. Bull Dog Bank

We have never seen the Deer figurine in gold, but it is possible.

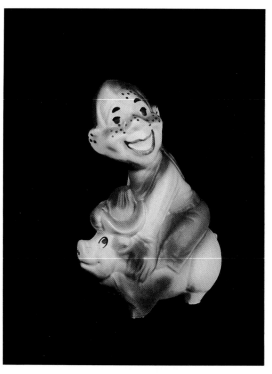

**Plate 334. Howdy Doody Bank
Marked USA Bob Smith**

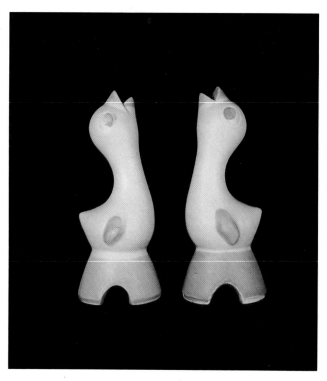

Plate 335. Pie Birds

**Plate 336. Sock Darners
Marked USA**

**Plate 337. Gold Goblets
Marked Hand Decorated 24 Karat Gold**

**Plate 338. Bucket Sugar Bowl
Marked USA**

**Plate 339. Bucket Sugar Bowl With Gold & Decals
Marked USA**

**Plate 340. Bucket Sugar Bowl
Marked Great
Northern USA 1042**

**Plate 341. Sunflower Sugar Bowl
Marked USA**

Plate 342. Clover Bud Sugar Bowl
Marked USA

Plate 343. Decorative Sugar Bowl
Marked USA

Plate 345. Pennsylvania Dutch – Tab Handle
Sugar Bowl
Marked USA

Plate 344. Pennsylvania Dutch – Jug Sugar
Marked USA

This Dutch tab handle sugar bowl was not made with a lid.

**Plate 346. Blue Embossed Design Sugar Bowl
Marked USA**

**Plate 347. Blue Jug Sugar
Marked USA**

Also available in different colors: green & yellow.

**Plate 348. Cottage Sugar Bowl
Marked USA 8**

**Plate 349. Fruit Sugar Bowl
Marked Shawnee 83**

Plate 350. Fruit Casserole
Marked Shawnee 83

Plate 351. Fruit Casserole
Gold Trim
Marked Shawnee 83

Plate 352. Green Basketweave
Utility Jar
Marked USA

Plate 353. Green Basketweave
Utility Jar With Gold & Decals
Marked USA

Plate 354. Blue Basketweave
Utility Jar
Marked USA

Plate 355. Blue Basketweave
Utility Jar With Gold & Decals
Marked USA

Plate 356. Green Basketweave
Utility Jar
Marked USA

**Plate 357. Green Basketweave
Utility Jar With Gold & Decals**

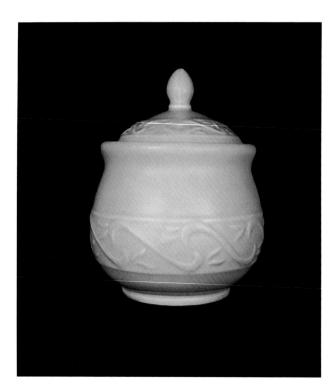

**Plate 358. Green Sugar
Embossed Design
Marked USA**

**Plate 359. Yellow Sugar Bowl
Flower & Fern
Marked USA**

Possibly in different colors.

**Plate 360. Green Sugar Bowl Flower & Fern
Marked USA**

Possibly in different colors, the small items in the snowflake design such as sugar bowls, creamers, and salt & peppers were given as premiums from Proctor & Gamble.

Plate 361. Yellow Snowflake Sugar Bowl
Marked USA

Plate 362. Salt Box
Fernware
Marked USA

Plate 362 and 363 are available in different colors.

Plate 364. Nesting Bowls – Snowflake
Marked USA

There are 5 sizes & colors in this Snowflake nesting bowl set, the two not shown are yellow & green.

Plate 363. Match Holder
Fernware
Marked USA

Plate 365. Tankards – Medallion Finish
Marked Shawnee USA 990 Pat. Pen.

Plate 366. Cigarette Box
Embossed Trademark
Marked USA

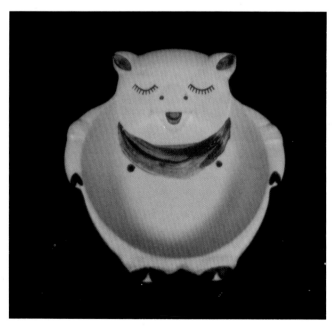

Plate 367. Pig Bowl
Marked USA

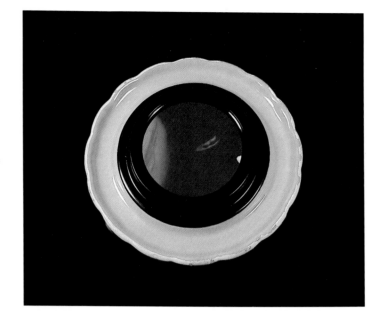

**Plate 368. Pink Elephant Head
with rubber gasket to protect head &
bottom and for a better seal**

Plate 369. Orientals – Singles & Double

Plaste 370. Spanish Dancers

Plate 371. Large Orientals Playing Mandolin

Plate 372. Small Orientals Playing Mandolin

Plate 373. Black Faces With Gold

Plate 374. Dark Natives
Gold Trim

Plate 375 & 376. Light Natives

Plate 377. Champ The Dog

Plate 378. Tube Base With Oriental

Plate 379. Victorians

Plate 380. Large White Casserole Marked 904

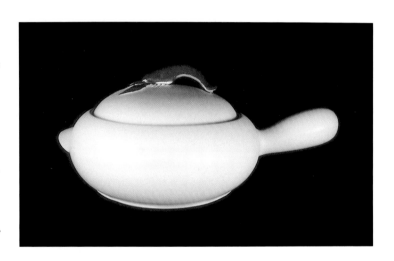

The white base on this casserole was a sample color. Very few of this color were produced.

Plate 381. Casseroles Small, Medium & Large Marked 900, 902 & 904

**Plate 382. Turquoise Sundial
Large & Medium
Marked 904 & 902**

These items are found with the stand and ceramic candle cup.

**Plate 383. Pink Sundial
Medium & Small
Marked 902 & 904**

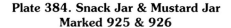

**Plate 384. Snack Jar & Mustard Jar
Marked 925 & 926**

"LOBSTER

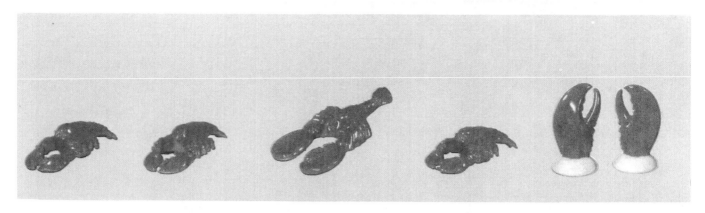

933 — Salt and Pepper Shakers
7¼" Long with Corks
3 Pairs to Ctn. Wt. 8 lbs.
$3.00 Pair

935 — Double Spoon Holder
8½" Long
6 Only to Ctn. Wt. 6 lbs.
$2.00 Each

932 — Hors d'oeuvre Holder
7¼" Long
6 Only to Ctn. Wt. 4 lbs.
$1.50 Each

905 — Salt and Pepper Shakers
5" High with Corks
6 Pairs to Ctn. Wt. 5½ lbs.
$2.00 Pair

921 — Salad, Soup or Chili Bowl
5¾" Diameter
12 Only to Ctn. Wt. 12 lbs.
$0.60 Each

922 — Salad or Spaghetti Bowl
14" Diameter
3 Only to Ctn. Wt. 23 lbs.
$4.50 Each

923 — Wood Spoon and Fork Set
12" Long
6 Sets to Ctn. Wt. 1½ lbs.
$1.90 Set

909 — Creamer Jug
13 Ounces
6 Only to Ctn. Wt. 6½ lbs.
$1.25 Each

928 — Handled Batter Bowl
8" Diameter
6 Only to Ctn. Wt. 18 lbs.
$2.00 Each

912 — Compartment Plate
11¾" Long
12 Only to Ctn. Wt. 40 lbs.
$1.50 Each

LOBSTER WARE IS AVAILABLE IN SATIN CHARCOAL GLAZE
(ILLUSTRATED) OR GLOSSY VAN DYKE BROWN GLAZE. EACH
ITEM LABELED.

bake and serve ware . . . "

911 — Mug
8 Ounces
12 Only to Ctn. Wt. 10 lbs.
$1.00 Each

927 — Covered Butter Dish
7¼" Long
6 Only to Ctn. Wt. 10½ lbs.
$2.00 Each

925 — Snack Jar or Bean Pot
40 Ounces
4 only to Ctn. Wt. 15 lbs.
$3.50 Each

907 — Covered Sugar
or Utility Jar
16 Ounces
6 Only to Ctn. Wt. 8 lbs.
$2.25 Each

926 — Covered Relish Pot
5½ Ounces
6 Only to Ctn. Wt. 4½ lbs.
$1.35 Each

904 — French Casserole
2-Quart
4 Only to Ctn. Wt. 17 lbs.
$4.50 Each

902 — French Casserole
16-Ounce
6 Only to Ctn. Wt. 13½ lbs.
$2.75 Each

900 — French Casserole
10-Ounce
6 Only to Ctn. Wt. 8½ lbs.
$2.25 Each

915 — Mixing Bowl or Open Baker
5" Diameter
12 Only to Ctn. Wt. 12 lbs.
$0.60 Each

917 — Mixing Bowl or Open Baker
7" Diameter
6 Only to Ctn. Wt. 12½ lbs.
$1.00 Each

919 — Mixing Bowl or Open Baker
9" Diameter
6 Only to Ctn. Wt. 18 lbs.
$1.65 Each

SEE PAGES 7-8 FOR NEWS MAT INFORMATION

SEE PAGE 9 FOR ASSORTMENT

"LOBSTER

913 — 8-Pc. Patio Plate and Mug Set
Composed of: 4 only 11¾" Compartment Plates; 4 only 8-oz. Mugs
1 Set to Ctn.   Wt. 16½ lbs. $10.00 Set

906 — 4-Pc. Range Set
Composed of: 1 Pr. Salt and Pepper Shakers;
1 only 16-oz. Covered Jar
Each Set individually boxed
4 Sets to Ctn. Wt. 12 lbs. $4.25 Set

901 — 8-Pc. French Casserole Set
Composed of:
4 only 10-oz. Covered Casseroles
Each Set individually boxed
4 Sets to Ctn. Wt. 23 lbs. $9.00 Set

910 — 3-Pc. Sugar and Creamer Set
Composed of: 1 only 16-oz. Covered Sugar;
1 only 13-oz. Creamer.
Each Set individually boxed
4 Sets to Ctn. Wt. 12 lbs. $3.50 Set

**LOBSTER WARE IS AVAILABLE IN SATIN CHARCOAL GLAZE
(ILLUSTRATED) OR GLOSSY VAN DYKE BROWN GLAZE. EACH
ITEM LABELED.**

bake and serve ware ... "

920 — 3-Pc. Bowl or Open Baker Set.
Composed of: 1 only 5" Bowl; 1 only 7" Bowl; 1 only 9" Bowl
Each Set individually boxed.   6 Sets to Ctn. Wt. 37½ lbs. $3.25 Set

924 — 9-Pc. Salad Set
Composed of: 6 only 5¾" Individual Bowls;
1 only 14" Salad Bowl; 1 pr. 12" Wood Fork and Spoon Set
1 Set to Ctn. Wt. 11 lbs. $10.00 Set

SEE PAGES 7-8 FOR NEWS MAT INFORMATION

SEE PAGE 9 FOR ASSORTMENT

Plate 385. Sugar Bowl
Marked 907

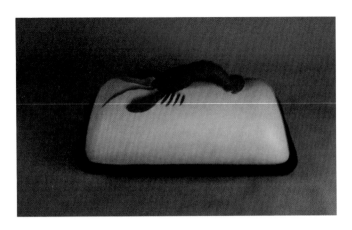

Plate 386. Butterdish
Marked 927

Plate 387. Lobster Pins
Marked Kenwood Ceramics Zanesville Ohio
Made To Hand Out At Pottery Shows

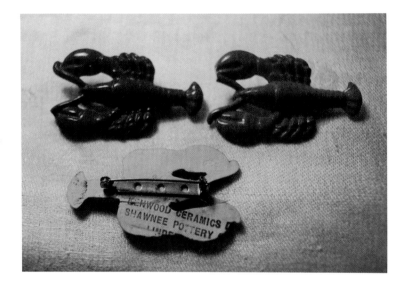

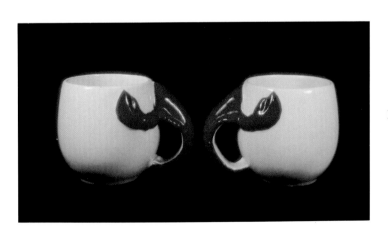

Plate 388. Mugs With Lobster Handles
Marked 911

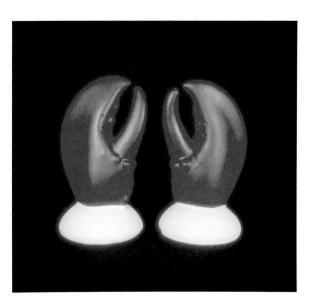

Plate 389. Claw Shakers

Plate 390. Lobster Shakers

Plate 391. Hors d'oeuvre Holder
With 25 Holes

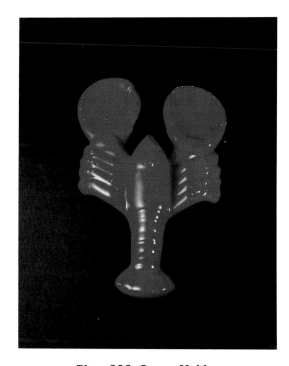

Plate 392. Spoon Holder

Plate 393. Lobster Handle Shakers – Brown

**Plate 394. Brown & Black Lobster Handle Creamers
Marked 909**

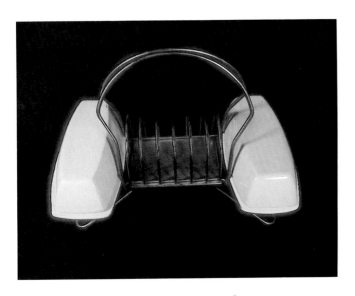

Plate 395. Pink Toastie Susan

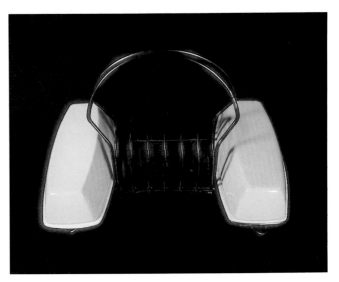

Plate 396. Turquoise Toastie Susan

Plate 397. Sausie Susan

Plate 398. Carafe On Stand

**Plate 399. Mixing Bowl with Medallion Lid
Marked Kenwood 940**

**Plate 400. Pyramid Clock
Medallion Finish**

Plate 401. Pink & Medallion Clock

Plate 402. Trellis Clock

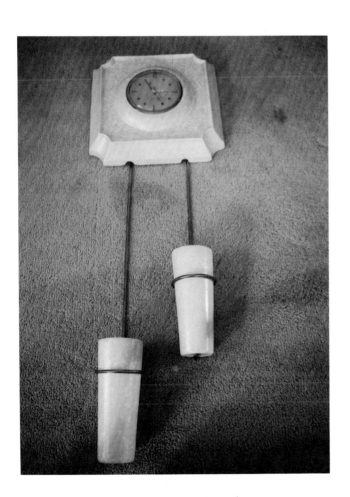

Plate 403. Granddaughter Clock

Valencia

In 1937, Shawnee Pottery designed a line of dinnerware for Sears Roebuck and Company that was called Valencia. It was designed by Louise Bauer, who designed for Shawnee from 1937 to 1939. Producing a dinnerware line was the brainchild of Addis E. Hull, president of Shawnee from 1937 to 1950. Miss Bauer submitted several sketches to Mr. Hull and the Sears Company buyers. The Valencia Sketches were chosen. Sears promoted the line by giving a starter set with each purchase of a new refrigerator. A complete line was then designed and produced during this time. Whether all items were produced is unknown. Plates, cups, saucers, syrup pitchers, water pitchers, salt & pepper sets, and candleholders have been found. Valencia was originally produced in four colors: yellow, blue, green, and tangerine. Later, maroon was added. Valencia was short lived with production ending in the early 1940's. Valencia can be identified by the fluting on the top and sides of the pieces. Some of the pieces are marked Valencia, some are marked USA, however most are not marked at all.

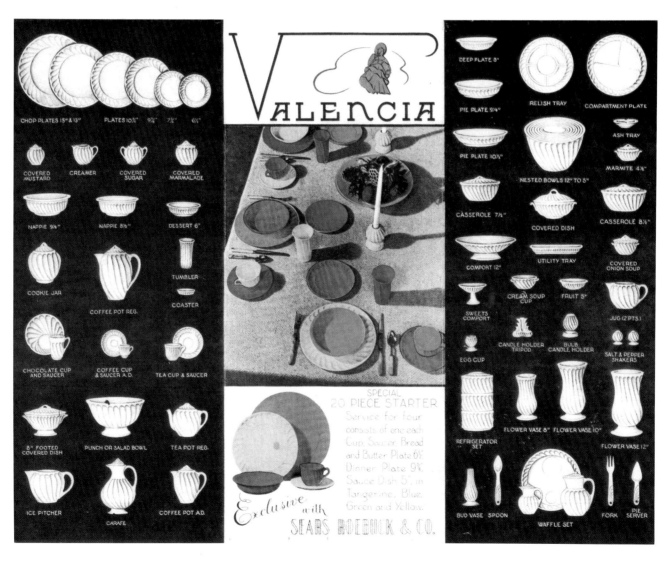

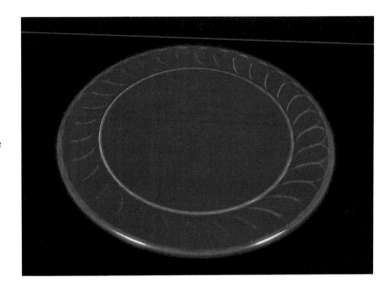

Plate 404. 13" Chop Plate

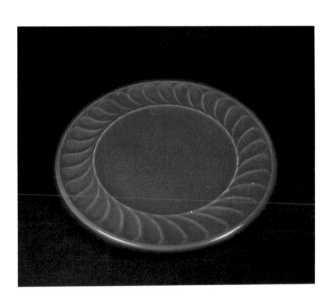

Plate 405. Blue 10" Plate

Plate 406. 13" Chop Plate

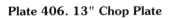

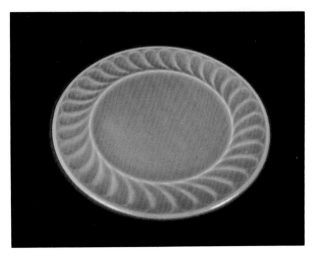

Plate 407. Green 10" Plate

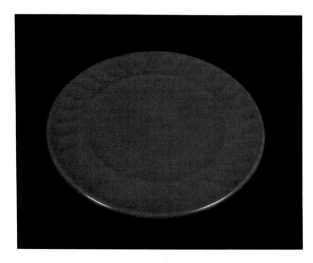

**Plate 408. Tangerine
10" Plate**

Plate 409. Yellow 10" Plate

**Plate 410. Tangerine
9½" Nappie**

Plate 411. Tangerine 8"
Deep Plate

Plate 412. Yellow 8½"
Nappie

Plate 413. Blue Sugar & Yellow Creamer
Marked Valencia

Plate 414. Green Ball Jug
Marked USA

Plate 415. Tangerine Ball Jug

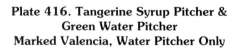

**Plate 416. Tangerine Syrup Pitcher &
Green Water Pitcher
Marked Valencia, Water Pitcher Only**

Corn Ware

One of Shawnee's best selling lines was the corn style dinnerware line. The corn line got its start around 1940 by Martha Holmes Breithaupt. She designed a few items, such as the water pitcher, creamer, sugar bowl, sugar shaker, large and small salt & pepper shakers, and a 30 ounce teapot. These items were hand decorated in a white & green glaze. The white corn items did not sell very well.

In 1946, Robert Heckman took the original corn designs and changed the production colors to a yellow & green glaze. The new color combination was named King Corn and proved to be a huge success. Other dinnerware type items were designed and produced. However, the sugar shaker from the original corn designs was not carried over and produced in the new corn line.

In 1947, Jess Parentice was hired by Shawnee and placed in charge of production and merchandising. He came from Butler Brothers, where he had become familiar with Shawnee as a buyer of the Smiley and Winnie items. He and Robert Heckman worked together to design and market the corn line in prepackaged sets. The King Corn line included such sets as: Polly Anne's Popcorn set, and the Town and Country Snack set.

Another color change came about in 1954 when Mr. John Bonistall was installed as president of Shawnee. The colors were changed to a darker green and a lighter yellow glaze. The King Corn line was then phased out. The items produced remained the same with more prepackaged sets being introduced. Examples of some of the prepackaged sets in the Queen Corn line include: the Mixing Bowl set, the Table set, the Place Setting set, and Corn Roast set.

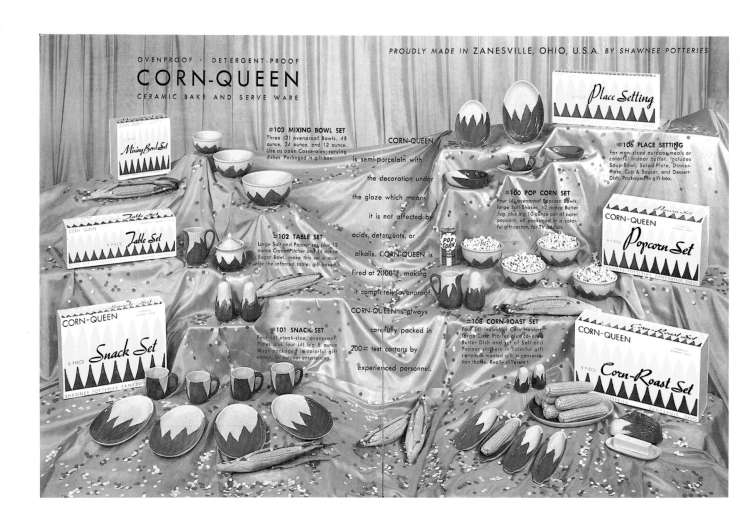

OVENPROOF · DETERGENT-PROOF

CORN-QUEEN

CERAMIC BAKE AND SERVE WARE

PROUDLY MADE IN ZANESVILLE, OHIO, U.S.A. BY SHAWNEE POTTERIES

#103 MIXING BOWL SET
Three (3) ovenproof Bowls, 48 ounce, 24 ounce, and 12 ounce. Use as open Casseroles, serving dishes. Packaged in gift-box.

CORN-QUEEN is semi-porcelain with the decoration under the glaze which means it is not affected by acids, detergents, or alkalis. CORN-QUEEN is fired at 2000°F. making it completely ovenproof. CORN-QUEEN is always carefully packed in 200# test cartons by experienced personnel.

#102 TABLE SET
Large Salt and Pepper set, plus 12 ounce Cream-Pitcher and 14 ounce Sugar Bowl, make this set a must for the informal table; gift-boxed.

#101 SNACK SET
Four (4) steak-size, ovenproof Plates plus four (4) big 8 ounce Mugs packaged in colorful gift carton, for outdoor entertaining.

#100 POP CORN SET
Four (4) ovenproof Popcorn Bowls, large Salt-Shaker, 12 ounce Butter Jug, plus big 10 ounce can of super popcorn, all packaged in a colorful gift carton, for TV-addicts.

#106 PLACE SETTING
For man-sized outdoor meals or colorful indoor buffet. Includes Soup-Bowl, Salad-Plate, Dinner-Plate, Cup & Saucer, and Dessert-Dish. Packaged in gift-box.

#108 CORN-ROAST SET
Four (4) individual Corn-Holders, large Corn-Platter, plus covered Butter Dish and set of Salt and Pepper shakers in colorful gift carton. A wanted gift, a conversation theme. Really different!!

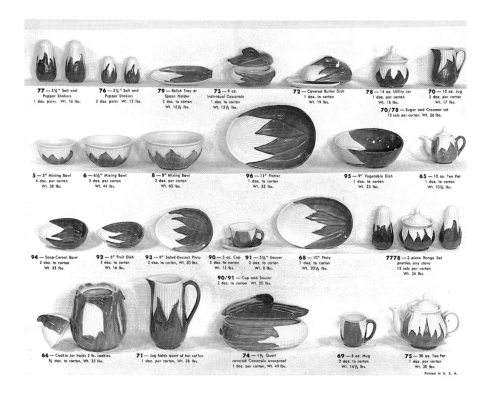

77 — 5½" Salt and Pepper Shakers 1 doz. pairs. Wt. 16 lbs.	76 — 3½" Salt and Pepper Shakers 2 doz. pairs. Wt. 12 lbs.	79 — Relish Tray or Spoon Holder 2 doz. to carton Wt. 16½ lbs.	73 — 9 oz. Individual Casserole 1 doz. to carton Wt. 15½ lbs.	72 — Covered Butter Dish 1 doz. to carton Wt. 19 lbs.	78 — 14 oz. Utility Jar 1 doz. per carton Wt. 18 lbs.	70 — 12 oz. Jug 2 doz. per carton Wt. 17 lbs.

70/78 — Sugar and Creamer set 12 sets per carton Wt. 26 lbs.

5 — 5" Mixing Bowl 4 doz. per carton Wt. 38 lbs.	6 — 6½" Mixing Bowl 3 doz. per carton Wt. 44 lbs.	8 — 8" Mixing Bowl 2 doz. per carton Wt. 60 lbs.	96 — 12" Platter 1 doz. to carton Wt. 25 lbs.	95 — 9" Vegetable Dish 1 doz. to carton Wt. 23 lbs.	65 — 10 oz. Tea Pot 1 doz. to carton Wt. 10½ lbs.

94 — Soup-Cereal Bowl 2 doz. to carton Wt. 28 lbs.	92 — 6" Fruit Dish 2 doz. to carton Wt. 16 lbs.	93 — 8" Salad-Dessert Plate 2 doz. to carton, Wt. 20 lbs.	90 — 5 oz. Cup 2 doz. to carton Wt. 12 lbs.	91 — 5½" Saucer 2 doz. to carton Wt. 8 lbs.	68 — 10" Plate 2 doz. to carton Wt. 20½ lbs.	7778 — 3 piece Range Set pretties any stove 12 sets per carton Wt. 34 lbs.

90/91 — Cup and Saucer 2 doz. to carton Wt. 20 lbs.

66 — Cookie Jar holds 2 lb. cookies ⅔ doz. to carton. Wt. 35 lbs.	71 — Jug holds quart of hot coffee 1 doz. per carton. Wt. 28 lbs.	74 — 1½ Quart covered Casserole ovenproof 1 doz. per carton. Wt. 49 lbs.	69 — 8 oz. Mug 2 doz. to carton Wt. 16½ lbs.	75 — 30 oz. Tea Pot 1 doz. per carton Wt. 30 lbs.

Printed in U. S. A.

**Plate 417. King Corn Cookie Jar
Marked #66**

**Plate 418. Queen Corn Cookie Jar
Marked #66**

**Plate 419. King 12" Platter &
10" Plate
Marked #96 & #68**

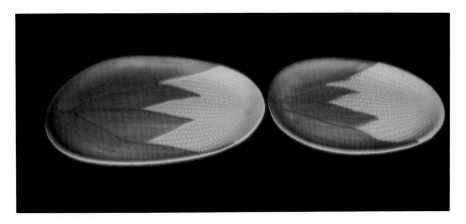

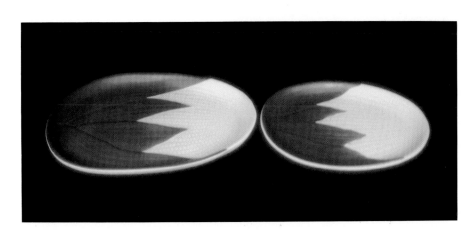

**Plate 420. Queen 12" Platter
& 10" Plate
Marked #96 & #68**

Plate 421. King Saucer & 8" Plate
Marked #91 & #93

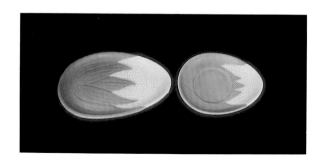

Plate 422. Queen 8" Plate & Saucer
Marked #93 & #91

Plate 423. King Mixing Bowls –
8", 6" & 5"
Marked Shawnee 8, 6 & 5

Plate 424. Queen Mixing
Bowls – 8", 6" & 5"
Marked Shawnee – 8, 6 & 5

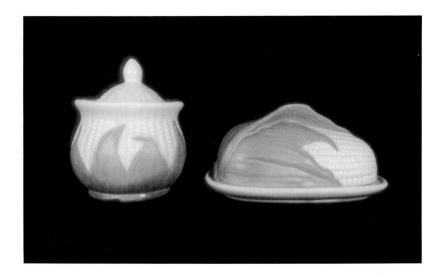

**Plate 425. King Sugar Bowl and
Butterdish
Marked #78 & #72**

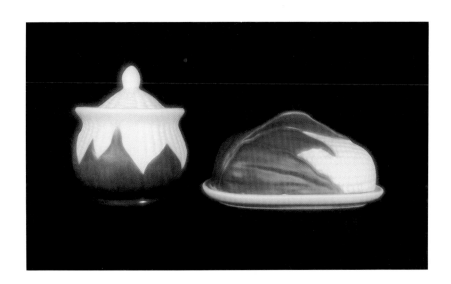

**Plate 426. Queen – Sugar
Bowl and Butterdish
Marked #78 & #72**

**Plate 427. King Shakers
Large & Small**

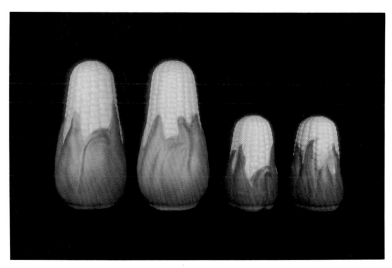

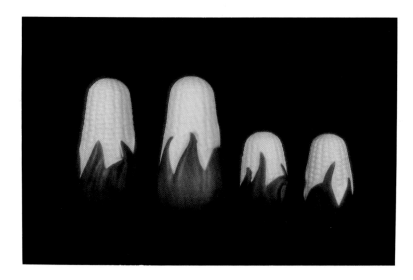

Plate 428. Queen Shakers
Large & Small

Plate 429. King Cup
& Mug
Marked #90 & #69

Plate 430. Queen Cup & Mug
Marked #90 & #69

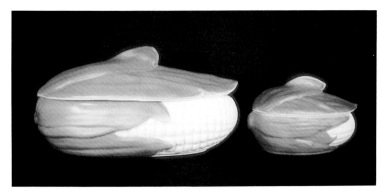

Plate 431. King – Large & Small
Casseroles
Marked #74 & #73

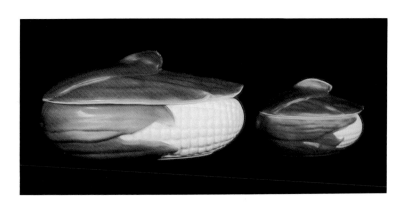

Plate 432. Queen Large
& Small Casseroles
Marked #74 & #73

Plate 433. King Vegetable
Bowl, Cereal Bowl & Fruit Dish
Mared #95, #94 & #92

Plate 434. Queen Vegetable
Bowl, Cereal Bowl & Fruit Dish
Marked #95, #94 & #92

Plate 435. King Pitcher & Creamer
Marked #71 & #70

Plate 436. Queen Pitcher & Creamer
Marked #71 & #70

Plate 437. King 30 oz. & 10 oz. Teapots
Marked #75 & #65

Plate 438. Queen 30 oz. & 10 oz. Teapots
Marked #75 & #65

Plate 439. King & Queen Relish
Marked #79

Plate 440. White Corn Sugar Shaker

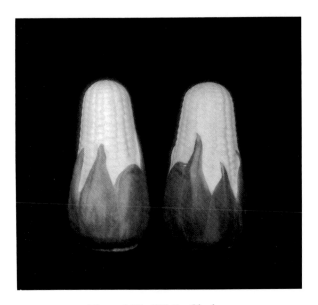

Plate 441. White Shakers

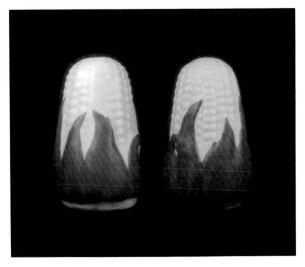

Plate 442. Small Shakers

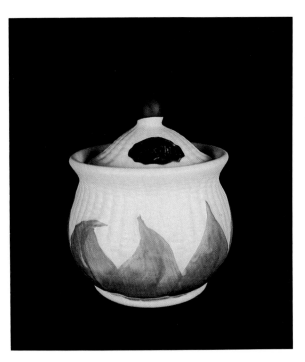

Plate 443. Sugar Bowl
Marked USA

Plate 444. White Corn Pitcher
Marked USA

Plate 445. White Creamer
Marked USA

Plate 446. White Corn 30 oz. Teapot
Marked USA

Plate 447. White Corn 30 oz. Teapot
Gold Trim
Marked USA

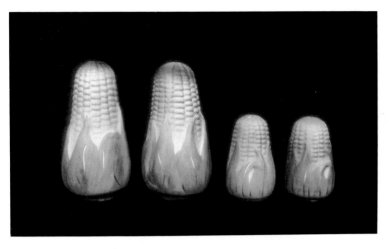

Plate 448. White Corn Shakers
Large & Small With Gold

Plate 449. White Corn Sugar Bowl
Gold Trim
Marked USA

Plate 451. Creamer With Gold
Marked USA

Plate 450. White Corn
Sugar Shaker With Gold

**Plate 452. White Corn Pitcher With Gold
Marked USA**

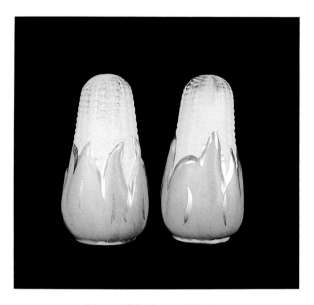

**Plate 453. Large Shakers
Gold Trim**

**Plate 455. King Corn Sugar & Creamer With Gold
Marked #78 – Sugar & #70 – Creamer**

**Plate 454. King Corn 30 oz. Teapot With Gold Trim
Marked #75**

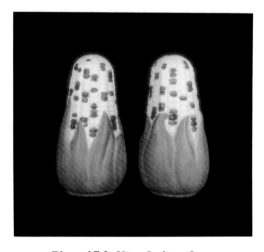

Plate 456. King Indian Corn

Price Guide

Plate 1	$50.00+	Plate 47	$250.00+
Plate 2	$50.00+	Plate 48	$250.00+
Plate 3.	$50.00+	Plate 49	$275.00+
Plate 4	$150.00+	Plate 50	$80.00+
Plate 5.	$175.00+	Plate 51	$75.00+
Plate 6	$150.00+	Plate 52	$75.00+
Plate 7	$150.00+	Plate 53a	$200.00+
Plate 8	$150.00+	Plate 53b	$250.00+
Plate 9	$200.00+	Plate 54	$125.00+
Plate 10	$200.00+	Plate 55	$225.00+
Plate 11	$200.00+	Plate 56	$200.00+
Plate 12	$250.00+	Plate 57	$300.00+
Plate 13	$250.00+	Plate 58	$150.00+
Plate 14	$275.00+	Plate 59	$300.00+
Plate 15	$300.00+	Plate 60	$75.00+
Plate 16	$400.00+	Plate 61	$80.00+
Plate 17	$225.00+	Plate 62	$75.00+
Plate 18a	$225.00+	Plate 63	$60.00+
Plate 18b	$275.00+	Plate 64	$150.00+
Plate 18c	$275.00+	Plate 65	$50.00+
Plate 18d	$275.00+	Plate 66	$80.00+
Plate 18e	$275.00+	Plate 67	$125.00+
Plate 19	$225.00+	Plate 68	$175.00+
Plate 20	$225.00+	Plate 69	$200.00+
Plate 21	$225.00+	Plate 70	$200.00+
Plate 22	$225.00+	Plate 71	$200.00+
Plate 23	$250.00+	Plate 72	$200.00+
Plate 24	$250.00+	Plate 73	$200.00+
Plate 25	$250.00+	Plate 74	$200.00+
Plate 26	$175.00+	Plate 75	$200.00+
Plate 27	$175.00+	Plate 76	$200.00+
Plate 28	$175.00+	Plate 77	$200.00+
Plate 29	$200.00+	Plate 79	$225.00+
Plate 30	$200.00+	Plate 80	$225.00+
Plate 31	$200.00+	Plate 81	$225.00+
Plate 32	$300.00+	Plate 82	$50.00+
Plate 33	$400.00+	Plate 83	$50.00+
Plate 34	$250.00+	Plate 84	$75.00+
Plate 35	$250.00+	Plate 85	$75.00+
Plate 36	$250.00+	Plate 86	$100.00+
Plate 37	$300.00+	Plate 87	$175.00+
Plate 38	$300.00+	Plate 88	$200.00+
Plate 39	$200.00+	Plate 89	$200.00+
Plate 40	$450.00+	Plate 90	$200.00+
Plate 41	$450.00+	Plate 91	$200.00+
Plate 42	$450.00+	Plate 92	$200.00+
Plate 43a	$450.00+	Plate 93	$200.00+
Plate 43b	$700.00+	Plate 94	$200.00+
Plate 44	$150.00+	Plate 95	$200.00+
Plate 45	$160.00+	Plate 96	$200.00+
Plate 46	$250.00+	Plate 97	$225.00+

Plate 98	$225.00+	Plate 153	$120.00-125.00
Plate 99	$100.00+	Plate 154	$115.00-120.00
Plate 100	$100.00+	Plate 155	$45.00-50.00
Plate 101	$400.00+	Plate 156	$45.00-50.00
Plate 102	$400.00+	Plate 157	$45.00-50.00
Plate 103	$450.00+	Plate 158	$45.00-50.00
Plate 104	$125.00+	Plate 159	$45.00-50.00
Plate 105	$200.00+	Plate 160	$55.00-60.00
Plate 106	$400.00+	Plate 161	$45.00-50.00
Plate 107	$75.00+	Plate 162	$85.00-90.00
Plate 108	$75.00+	Plate 163	$80.00-85.00
Plate 109	$75.00+	Plate 164	$85.00-90.00
Plate 110	$75.00+	Plate 165	$100.00-105.00
Plate 111	$150.00+	Plate 166	$45.00-50.00
Plate 112	$50.00+	Plate 167	$40.00-45.00
Plate 113	$50.00+	Plate 168	$40.00-45.00
Plate 114	$100.00+	Plate 169	$40.00-45.00
Plate 115	$100.00+	Plate 170	$65.00-70.00
Plate 116	$100.00+	Plate 171	$150.00-155.00
Plate 117	$75.00+	Plate 172	$60.00-65.00
Plate 118	$75.00+	Plate 173	$45.00-50.00
Plate 119	$50.00+	Plate 174	$225.00-250.00
Plate 120	$50.00+	Plate 175	$10.00-12.00
Plate 121	$50.00+	Plate 176	$80.00-85.00
Plate 122	$60.00+	Plate 177	$140.00-145.00
Plate 123	$60.00	Plate 178	$140.00-145.00
Plate 124	$85.00-90.00	Plate 179	$140.00-145.00
Plate 125	$85.00-90.00	Plate 180	$45.00-50.00
Plate 126	$95.00-100.00	Plate 181	$50.00-55.00
Plate 127	$100.00-105.00	Plate 182	$40.00-45.00
Plate 128	$145.00-150.00	Plate 183	$40.00-45.00
Plate 129	$145.00-150.00	Plate 184	$35.00-40.00
Plate 130	$145.00-150.00	Plate 185	$55.00-60.00
Plate 131	$65.00-70.00	Plate 186	$25.00-27.00
Plate 132	$145.00-150.00	Plate 187	$15.00-17.00
Plate 133	$145.00-150.00	Plate 188	$15.00-17.00
Plate 134	$145.00-150.00	Plate 189	$65.00-70.00
Plate 135	$150.00-155.00	Plate 190	$80.00-85.00
Plate 136	$145.00-150.00	Plate 191	$55.00-60.00
Plate 137	$250.00-275.00	Plate 192	$55.00-60.00
Plate 138	$85.00-90.00	Plate 193	$55.00-60.00
Plate 139	$85.00-90.00	Plate 194	$85.00-90.00
Plate 140	$150.00-155.00	Plate 195	$85.00-90.00
Plate 141	$160.00-165.00	Plate 196	$85.00-90.00
Plate 142	$150.00-155.00	Plate 197	$85.00-90.00
Plate 143	$150.00-155.00	Plate 198	$85.00-90.00
Plate 144	$75.00-80.00	Plate 199	$85.00-90.00
Plate 145	$125.00-130.00	Plate 200	$85.00-90.00
Plate 146	$85.00-90.00	Plate 201	$85.00-90.00
Plate 147	$140.00-145.00	Plate 202	$85.00-90.00
Plate 148	$90.00-95.00	Plate 203	$50.00-55.00
Plate 149	$75.00-80.00	Plate 204	$85.00-95.00
Plate 150	$90.00-95.00	Plate 205	$27.00-30.00
Plate 151	$65.00-70.00	Plate 206	$55.00-60.00
Plate 152	$100.00-105.00	Plate 207	$55.00-60.00

Plate 208	$42.00-45.00
Plate 209	$45.00-50.00
Plate 210	$80.00-85.00
Plate 211	$80.00-85.00
Plate 212	$155.00-160.00
Plate 213	$47.00-50.00
Plate 214	$47.00-50.00
Plate 215	$27.00-30.00
Plate 216	`$50.00-55.00
Plate 217	$47.00-50.00
Plate 218	$27.00-30.00
Plate 219	$27.00-30.00
Plate 220	$27.00-30.00
Plate 221	$27.00-30.00
Plate 222	$50.00-55.00
Plate 223	$22.00-25.00
Plate 224	$35.00-38.00
Plate 225	$35.00-38.00
Plate 226	$43.00-45.00
Plate 227	$47.00-50.00
Plate 228	$32.00-35.00
Plate 229	$55.00-60.00
Plate 230	$55.00-60.00
Plate 231	$55.00-60.00
Plate 232	$55.00-60.00
Plate 233	$22.00-25.00
Plate 234	$45.00-47.00
Plate 235	$30.00-33.00
Plaet 236	$55.00-60.00
Plate 237	$55.00-60.00
Plate 238	$25.00-27.00
Plate 239	$20.00-23.00
Plate 240	$37.00-40.00
Plate 241	$37.00-40.00
Plate 242	$55.00-60.00
Plate 243	$17.00-20.00
Plate 244	$37.00-40.00
Plate 245	$17.00-20.00
Plate 246	$37.00-40.00
Plate 247	$32.00-35.00
Plate 248	$12.00-15.00
Plate 249	$37.00-40.00
Plate 250	$37.00-40.00
Plate 251	$12.00-15.00
Plate 252	$27.00-30.00
Plate 253	$12.00-15.00
Plate 254	$32.00-35.00
Plate 255	$12.00-15.00
Plate 256	$37.00-40.00
Plate 257	$12.00-15.00
Plate 258	$27.00-30.00
Plate 259	$27.00-30.00
Plate 260	$12.00-15.00
Plate 261	$27.00-30.00
Plate 262	$80.00-85.00
Plate 263	$27.00-30.00
Plate 265	$12.00-15.00
Plate 265	$65.00-70.00
Plate 266	$65.00-70.00
Plate 267	$65.00-70.00
Plate 268	$135.00-140.00
Plate 269	$135.00-140.00
Plate 270	$170.00-175.00
Plate 271	$170.00-175.00
Plate 272	$65.00-70.00
Plate 273	$65.00-70.00
Plate 274	$135.00-140.00
Plate 275	$130.00-135.00
Plate 276	$170.00-175.00
Plate 277	$100.00-105.00
Plate 278	$80.00-85.00
Plate 279	$80.00-85.00
Plate 280	$80.00-85.00
Plate 281	$130.00-135.00
Plate 282	$90.00-95.00
Plate 283	$80.00-85.00
Plate 284	$75.00-80.00
Plate 285	$70.00-75.00
Plate 286	$65.00-70.00
Plate 287	$65.00-70.00
Plate 288	$95.00-100.00
Plate 289	$35.00-40.00
Plate 290	$65.00-70.00
Plate 291	$125.00-130.00
Plate 292	$60.00-65.00
Plate 293	$125.00-130.00
Plate 294	$37.00-40.00
Plate 295	$50.00-55.00
Plate 296	$125.00-130.00
Plate 297	$42.00-45.00
Plate 298	$65.00-70.00
Plate 299	$27.00-30.00
Plate 300	$47.00-50.00
Plate 301	$27.00-30.00
Plate 302	$47.00-50.00
Plate 303	$35.00-38.00
Plate 304	$45.00-50.00
Plate 305	$27.00-30.00
Plate 306	$27.00-30.00
Plate 307	$27.00-30.00
Plate 308	$27.00-30.00
Plate 309	$45.00-50.00
Plate 310	$45.00-50.00
Plate 311	$22.00-25.00
Plate 312	$22.00-25.00
Plate 313	$22.00-25.00
Plate 314	$22.00-25.00
Plate 315	$22.00-25.00
Plate 316	$22.00-25.00
Plate 317	$250.00-275.00

Plate 318.	$37.00-40.00
Plate 319	$75.00-80.00
Plate 320	$37.00-40.00
Plate 321	$75.00-80.00
Plate 322	$37.00-40.00
Plate 323	$75.00-80.00
Plate 324	$37.00-40.00
Plate 325	$75.00-80.00
Plate 326	$75.00-80.00
Plate 327	$37.00-40.00
Plate 328	$75.00-80.00
Plate 329	$37.00-40.00
Plate 330	$75.00-80.00
Plate 331	$65.00-70.00
Plate 332	$85.00-90.00
Plate 333	$90.00-95.00
Plate 334	$300.00-310.00
Plate 335	$27.00-30.00
Plate 336	$27.00-30.00
Plate 337	$45.00-50.00
Plate 338	$27.00-30.00
Plate 339	$55.00-60.00
Plate 340	$37.00-40.00
Plate 341	$27.00-30.00
Plate 342	$37.00-40.00
Plate 343	$25.00-27.00
Plate 344	$47.00-50.00
Plate 345	$55.00-60.00
Plate 346	$22.00-25.00
Plate 347	$27.00-30.00
Plate 348	$125.00-130.00
Plate 349	$32.00-35.00
Plate 350	$50.00-55.00
Plate 351.	$70.00-75.00
Plate 352	$55.00-60.00
Plate 353	$80.00-85.00
Plate 354	$60.00-65.00
Plate 355	$90.00-95.00
Plate 356	$60.00-65.00
Plate 357	$90.00-95.00
Plate 358	$22.00-25.00
Plate 359	$17.00-20.00
Plate 360	$12.00-15.00
Plate 361	$12.00-15.00
Plate 362	$32.00-35.00
Plate 363	$22.00-25.00
Plate 364 7"	$15.00-17.00
6"	$12.00-15.00
5"	$10.00-12.00
Plate 365	$22.00-25.00
Plate 366	$50.00-55.00
Plate 367	$80.00-85.00
Plate 369 single (pr)	$37.00-40.00
double (pr)	$45.00-47.00

Plate 370 (pr)	$37.00-40.00
Plate 371	$37.00-40.00
Plate 372	$37.00-40.00
Plate 373	$145.00-155.00
Plate 374	$125.00-130.00
Plate 375 & 376	$190.00-200.00
Plate 377	$17.00-20.00
Plate 378	$12.00-15.00
Plate 379	$32.00-35.00
Plate 380	$60.00-65.00
Plate 381 small	$12.00-15.00
medium	$22.00-25.00
large	$35.00-37.00
Plate 382 large	$47.00-50.00
medium	37.00-40.00
Plate 383 medium	$27.00-30.00
large	$35.00-37.00
Plate 384 snack jar	$175.00-180.00
mustard jar	$37.00-40.00
Plate 385	$22.00-25.00
Plate 386	$60.00-65.00
Plate 387	$22.00-25.00
Plate 388	$37.00-40.00
Plate 389	$17.00-20.00
Plate 390	$60.00-65.00
Plate 391	$75.00-80.00
Plate 392	$75.00-80.00
Plate 393	$42.00-45.00
Plate 394	$47.00-50.00
Plate 395	$60.00-65.00
Plate 396	$60.00-65.00
Plate 397	$60.00-65.00
Plate 398	$47.00-50.00
Plate 399	$37.00-40.00
Plate 400	$60.00-65.00
Plate 401	$47.00-50.00
Plate 402	$47.00-50.00
Plate 403	$75.00-80.00
Plate 404	$10.00-12.00
Plate 405	$5.00-7.00
Plate 406	$10.00-12.00
Plate 407	$5.00-7.00
Plate 408	$5.00-7.00
Plate 409	$5.00-7.00
Plate 410	$7.00-10.00
Plate 411	$7.00-10.00
Plate 412	$7.00-10.00
Plate 413	$7.00-10.00
Plate 414	$15.00-17.00
Plate 415	$15.00-17.00
Plate 416 syrup pitcher	$12.00-15.00
water pitcher	$17.00-20.00
Plate 417	$135.00-145.00
Plate 418	$145.00-155.00

Plate 419	12" platter	$42.00-45.00
	10" platter	$27.00-30.00
Plate 420	12" platter	$42.00-45.00
	10" platter	$27.00-30.00
Plate 421	saucer	$10.00-12.00
	plate	$22.00-25.00
Plate 422	plate	$22.00-25.00
	saucer	$12.00-15.00
Plate 423	8"	$32.00-35.00
	6"	$27.00-30.00
	5"	$22.00-25.00
Plate 424	8"	$32.00-35.00
	6"	$27.00-30.00
	5"	$22.00-25.00
Plate 425	#78	$27.00-30.00
	#72	$47.00-50.00
Plate 426	#78	$27.00-30.00
	#72	$47.00-50.00
Plate 427	large	$22.00-25.00
	small	$15.00-17.00
Plate 428	large	$22.00-25.00
	small	$15.00-17.00
Plate 429	cup	$27.00-30.00
	mug	$42.00-45.00
Plate 430	cup	$27.00-30.00
	mug	$42.00-45.00
Plate 431	#74	$32.00-35.00
	#73	$47.00-50.00
Plate 432	#74	$37.00-40.00
	#73	$47.00-50.00
Plate 433	#95	$32.00-35.00
	#94	$42.00-45.00
	#92	$37.00-40.00

Plate 434	#95	$32.00-35.00
	#94	$42.00-45.00
	#92	$37.00-40.00
Plate 435	#71	$60.00-65.00
	#70	$22.00-25.00
Plate 436	#71	$60.00-65.00
	#70	$22.00-25.00
Plate 437	#75	$65.00-70.00
	#65	$115.00-120.00
Plate 438	#75	$65.00-70.00
	#65	$115.00-120.00
Plate 439		$15.00-17.00
Plate 440		$55.00-60.00
Plate 441		$27.00-30.00
Plate 442		$22.00-25.00
Plate 443		$27.00-30.00
Plate 444		$65.00-70.00
Plate 445		$25.00-27.00
Plate 446		$55.00-60.00
Plate 447		$115.00-120.00
Plate 448	large	$47.00-50.00
	small	$32.00-35.00
Plate 449		$55.00-60.00
Plate 450		$85.00-90.00
Plate 451		$55.00-60.00
Plate 452		$95.00-100.00
Plate 453		$70.00-75.00
Plate 454		$145.00-150.00
Plate 455	#78	$75.00-80.00
	#70	$75.00-80.00
Plate 456		$60.00-65.00

Lobster Ware

ITEM DESCRIPTION	ITEM NUMBER	PRICE
French Casserole 10 oz.	900	$12.00-15.00
8 Pc. French Casserole Set	901	$65.00-70.00
French Casserole 16 oz	902	$22.00-25.00
French Casserole 2 qt.	904	$35.00-37.00
Claw Shakers	905	$17.00-20.00
4 Pc. Range Set	906	$65.00-70.00
Covered Sugar or Utility Jar	907	$22.00-25.00
3 Pc. Sugar and Creamer Set	910	$85.00-90.00
Mug	911	$37.00-40.00
Compartment Plate	912	$25.00-27.00
8 Pc. Patio Plate and Mug Set	913	$275.00-285.00
Mixing Bowl or Open Baker	915	$12.00-15.00
Mixing Bowl or Open Baker	917	$17.00-20.00
Mixing Bowl or Open Baker	919	$20.00-22.00
3 Pc. Bowl or Open Baker Set	920	$55.00-60.00
Creamer Jug	921	$47.00-50.00
Salad or Spaghetti Bowl	922	$30.00-35.00
Wood Spoon and Fork Set	923	$7.00-10.00
9 Pc. Salad Set	924	$130.00-135.00
Snack Jar or Bean Pot	925	$175.00-185.00
Covered Relish Pot	926	$37.00-40.00
Covered Butter Dish	927	$60.00-65.00
Handled Batter Bowl	928	$25.00-27.00
Hors d' oeuvre Holder	932	$75.00-80.00
Full-Body Shakers	933	$60.00-65.00
Double Spoon Holder	935	$75.00-80.00

Valencia

Tea Cups	$5.00-7.00
Tea Saucers	$4.00-6.00
Plate 10¾"	$5.00-7.00
Plate 9¾"	$5.00-7.00
Plate 7¾"	$4.00-6.00
Plate 6½"	$4.00-6.00
Deep Plate 8"	$7.00-10.00
Cream Soup Cup	$3.00-5.00
Covered Onion Soup	$7.00-10.00
Fruit 5"	$3.00-5.00
Dessert 6"	$5.00-7.00
Coffee Cup A.D.	$5.00-7.00
Coffee Saucer A.D.	$3.00-5.00
Chocolate Mug 7 oz.	$5.00-7.00
Chocolate Saucer 8"	$10.00-12.00
Chop Dish 15"	$12.00-15.00
Chop Dish 13"	$10.00-12.00
Nappie 9½"	$7.00-10.00
Nappie 8½"	$7.00-10.00
Covered Vegetable Dish 9½"	$15.00-17.00
Footed Covered Dish 8"	$15.00-17.00
Punch or Salad Bowl 12'	$17.00-20.00
Tom & Jerry Mug (Not illus.)	$5.00-7.00
Compartment Plate 11½"	$15.00-17.00
Sugar Bowl Covered	$5.00-7.00
Creamer	$3.00-5.00
Coffee Pot A.D.	$25.00-27.00
Coffee Pot Regular	$30.00-32.00
Teapot 8 cup	$17.00-20.00
Ice Pitcher 2 quart	$15.00-17.00
Jug 2 pint	$12.00-15.00
Carafe 3 pint	$25.00-27.00
Salt & Pepper Shakers	$5.00-7.00
Covered Mustard Jar	$5.00-7.00
Covered Marmalade Jar	$7.00-10.00
Covered Marmite 4½"	$7.00-10.00
Utility Tray 10½"	$3.00-5.00
Egg Cup	$3.00-5.00
Tumbler 10 oz.	$5.00-7.00
Coaster	$3.00-5.00
Comport or Console Bowl 12"	$10.00-12.00
Candle Holder Tripod	$5.00-7.00
Candle Holder Bulb	$3.00-5.00
Sweets Comport 7"	$5.00-7.00
Ash Tray	$3.00-5.00
Bud Vase	$3.00-5.00
Flower Vase 8"	$5.00-7.00
Flower Vase 10"	$7.00-10.00
Flower Vase 12"	$10.00-12.00

Valencia (Con't)

Mixing Bowl 12"	$18.00-20.00
Mixing Bowl 11"	$16.00-18.00
Mixing Bowl 10"	$14.00-16.00
Mixing Bowl 9"	$12.00-14.00
Mixing Bowl 8"	$10.00-12.00
Mixing Bowl 7"	$8.00-10.00
Mixing Bowl 6"	$8.00-10.00
Mixing Bowl 5"	$8.00-10.00
Relish Tray, Compartment	$17.00-20.00
5 Piece Waffle Set	
Plate	$17.00-20.00
Water Pitcher with Lid	$22.00-25.00
Syrup Pitcher with Lid	$15.00-17.00
Cookie Jar	$35.00-40.00
Baking Pie Plate 9¼"	$7.00-10.00
Baking Pie Plate 10½"	$10.00-12.00
Covered Casserole 7½"	$10.00-12.00
Covered Casserole 8½"	$15.00-17.00
3 Piece Refrigerator Set	$27.00-30.00
Spoon 9½"	$5.00-7.00
Fork 9½"	$7.00-10.00
Pie Server 9"	$10.00-12.00

King Corn Sets
(Price Per Set)

#100 Polly Ann's Pop Corn Set $175.00-185.00
#101 Town & Country Snack Set $190.00-200.00

Queen Corn Sets

#100 Popcorn Set $130.00-140.00
#101 Snack Set $150.00-150.00
#102 Table Set $40.00-50.00
#103 Mixing Bowl Set $80.00-90.00
#106 Place Setting $150.00-160.00
#108 Corn Roast Set $100.00-110.00

Books on Antiques and Collectibles

Most of the following books are available from your local book seller or antique dealer, or on loan from your public library. If you are unable to locate certain titles in your area you may order by mail from COLLECTOR BOOKS, P.O. Box 3009, Paducah, KY 42002-3009. This is only a partial listing of the books on antiques that are available from Collector Books. Add $2.00 for postage for the first book ordered and $.30 for each additional book. Include item number, title and price when ordering. Allow 14 to 21 days for delivery. All books are well illustrated and contain current values.

BOOKS ON GLASS AND POTTERY

1810	American Art Glass, Shuman	$29.95
2016	Bedroom & Bathroom Glassware of the Depression Years	$19.95
1312	Blue & White Stoneware, McNerney	$9.95
1959	Blue Willow, 2nd Ed., Gaston	$14.95
1627	Children's Glass Dishes, China & Furniture II, Lechler	$19.95
2270	Collectible Glassware from the 40's, 50's, & 60's, Florence	$19.95
1892	Collecting Royal Haeger, Garmon	$19.95
2352	Collector's Ency. of Akro Agate Glassware, Florence	$14.95
1373	Collector's Ency of American Dinnerware, Cunningham	$24.95
2272	Collector's Ency. of California Pottery, Chipman	$24.95
2133	Collector's Ency. of Cookie Jars, Roerig	$24.95
2273	Collector's Ency. of Depression Glass, 10th Ed., Florence	$19.95
2209	Collector's Ency. of Fiesta, 7th Ed., Huxford	$19.95
1439	Collector's Ency. of Flow Blue China, Gaston	$19.95
1915	Collector's Ency. of Hall China, 2nd Ed., Whitmyer	$19.95
2210	Collector's Ency. of Limoges Porcelain, 2nd Ed., Gaston	$24.95
2334	Collector's Ency. of Majolica Pottery, Katz-Marks	$19.95
1358	Collector's Ency. of McCoy Pottery, Huxford	$19.95
1039	Collector's Ency. of Nippon Porcelain I, Van Patten	$19.95
2089	Collector's Ency. of Nippon Porcelain II, Van Patten	$24.95
1665	Collector's Ency. of Nippon Porcelain III, Van Patten	$24.95
1447	Collector's Ency. of Noritake, Van Patten	$19.95
1037	Collector's Ency. of Occupied Japan I, Florence	$14.95
1038	Collector's Ency. of Occupied Japan II, Florence	$14.95
2088	Collector's Ency. of Occupied Japan III, Florence	$14.95
2019	Collector's Ency. of Occupied Japan IV, Florence	$14.95
2335	Collector's Ency. of Occupied Japan V, Florence	$14.95
1034	Collector's Ency. of Roseville Pottery, Huxford	$19.95
1035	Collector's Ency. of Roseville Pottery, 2nd Ed., Huxford	$19.95
2339	Collector's Guide to Shawnee Pottery, Vanderbilt	$19.95
1425	Cookie Jars, Westfall	$9.95
2275	Czechoslovakian Glass & Collectibles, Barta	$16.95
2024	Kitchen Glassware of the Depression Years, 4th Ed., Florence	$19.95
2379	Lehner's Ency. of U.S. Marks on Pottery, Porcelain & Clay	$24.95
1438	Oil Lamps II, Thuro	$19.95
2345	Portland Glass, Ladd	$24.95
1670	Red Wing Collectibles, DePasquale	$9.95
1440	Red Wing Stoneware, DePasquale	$9.95
1958	So. Potteries Blue Ridge Dinnerware, 3rd Ed., Newbound	$14.95
2221	Standard Carnival Glass, 3rd Ed., Edwards	$24.95
2222	Standard Carnival Glass Price Guide, 1991, 8th Ed., Edwards	$7.95
2347	Standard Opalescent Glass Price Guide, Edwards	$9.95
1848	Very Rare Glassware of the Depression Years, Florence	$24.95
2140	Very Rare Glassware of the Depression Years, Second Series	$24.95
2224	World of Salt Shakers, 2nd Ed., Lechner	$24.95

BOOKS ON DOLLS & TOYS

2079	Barbie Fashion, Vol. 1, 1959-1967, Eames	$24.95
1514	Character Toys & Collectibles 1st Series, Longest	$19.95
1750	Character Toys & Collectibles, 2nd Series, Longest	$19.95
2021	Collectible Male Action Figures, Manos	$14.95
1529	Collector's Ency. of Barbie Dolls, DeWein	$19.95
2151	Collector's Guide to Tootsietoys, Richter	$16.95
1067	Madame Alexander Collector's Dolls, Smith	$19.95
2342	Madame Alexander Price Guide #17, Smith	$9.95
1540	Modern Toys, 1930-1980, Baker	$19.95
2343	Patricia Smith's Doll Values Antique to Modern, 8th ed	$12.95
1886	Stern's Guide to Disney	$14.95
2139	Stern's Guide to Disney, 2nd Series	$14.95

1513	Teddy Bears & Steiff Animals, Mandel	$9.95
1817	Teddy Bears & Steiff Animals, 2nd, Mandel	$19.95
2084	Teddy Bears, Annalees & Steiff Animals, 3rd, Mandel	$19.95
2028	Toys, Antique & Collectible, Longest	$14.95
1808	Wonder of Barbie, Manos	$9.95
1430	World of Barbie Dolls, Manos	$9.95

OTHER COLLECTIBLES

2280	Advertising Playing Cards, Grist	$16.95
1457	American Oak Furniture, McNerney	$9.95
2269	Antique Brass & Copper, Gaston	$16.95
2333	Antique & Collectible Marbles, Grist, 3rd Ed.	$9.95
1712	Antique & Collectible Thimbles, Mathis	$19.95
1880	Antique Iron, McNerney	$9.95
1748	Antique Purses, Holiner	$19.95
1868	Antique Tools, Our American Heritage, McNerney	$9.95
1426	Arrowheads & Projectile Points, Hothem	$7.95
1278	Art Nouveau & Art Deco Jewelry, Baker	$9.95
1714	Black Collectibles, Gibbs	$19.95
1128	Bottle Pricing Guide, 3rd Ed., Cleveland	$7.95
1751	Christmas Collectibles, Whitmyer	$19.95
1752	Christmas Ornaments, Johnston	$19.95
2132	Collector's Ency. of American Furniture, Vol. I, Swedberg	$24.95
2271	Collector's Ency. of American Furniture, Vol. II, Swedberg	$24.95
2018	Collector's Ency. of Graniteware, Greguire	$24.95
2083	Collector's Ency. of Russel Wright Designs, Kerr	$19.95
2336	Collector's Guide to Antique Radios 2nd Ed., Bunis	$17.95
1916	Collector's Guide to Art Deco, Gaston	$14.95
1537	Collector's Guide to Country Baskets, Raycraft	$9.95
1962	Collector's Guide to Decoys, Huxford	$14.95
2337	Collector's Guide to Decoys, Book II, Huxford	$16.95
2338	Collector's Guide to Disneyana, Longest & Stern	$24.95
1441	Collector's Guide to Post Cards, Wood	$9.95
2276	Decoys, Kangas	$24.95
1629	Doorstops, Id & Values, Betoria	$9.95
1716	Fifty Years of Fashion Jewelry, Baker	$19.95
2213	Flea Market Trader, 7th Ed., Huxford	$9.95
1755	Furniture of the Depression Era, Swedberg	$19.95
2081	Guide to Collecting Cookbooks, Allen	$14.95
2340	Collector's Guide to Easter Collectibles, Burnett	$16.95
2278	Grist's Machine Made & Contemporary Marbles	$9.95
1424	Hatpins & Hatpin Holders, Baker	$9.95
1181	100 Years of Collectible Jewelry, Baker	$9.95
2023	Keen Kutter Collectibles, 2nd Ed., Heuring	$14.95
2216	Kitchen Antiques - 1790–1940, McNerney	$14.95
1965	Pine Furniture, Our Am. Heritage, McNerney	$14.95
2080	Price Guide to Cookbooks & Recipe Leaflets, Dickinson	$9.95
2026	Railroad Collectibles, 4th Ed., Baker	$14.95
1632	Salt & Pepper Shakers, Guarnaccia	$9.95
1888	Salt & Pepper Shakers II, Guarnaccia	$14.95
2220	Salt & Pepper Shakers III, Guarnaccia	$14.95
2281	Schroeder's Antiques Price Guide, 10th Ed.	$12.95
2346	Sheet Music Reference & Price Guide, Patik	$18.95
2096	Silverplated Flatware, 4th Ed., Hagan	$14.95
2277	Standard Baseball Card Pr. Gd., Florence	$9.95
2348	20th Century Fashionable Plastic Jewelry, Baker	$19.95
2223	Wanted to Buy	$9.95
1885	Victorian Furniture, McNerney	$9.95
2349	Value Guide to Baseball Collectibles, Raycraft	$16.95

Schroeder's Antiques Price Guide

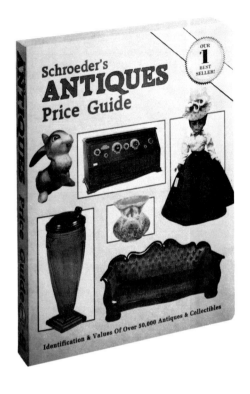

Schroeder's Antiques Price Guide has become THE household name in the antiques & collectibles field. Our team of editors work year-round with more than 200 contributors to bring you our #1 best-selling book on antiques & collectibles.

With more than 50,000 items identified & priced, Schroeder's is a must for the collector & dealer alike. If it merits the interest of today's collector, you'll find it in Schroeder's. Each subject is represented with histories and background information. In addition, hundreds of sharp original photos are used each year to illustrate not only the rare and unusual, but the everyday "fun-type" collectibles as well -- not postage stamp pictures, but large close-up shots that show important details clearly.

Our editors compile a new book each year. Never do we merely change prices. Accuracy is our primary aim. Prices are gathered over the entire year previous to publication, from ads and personal contacts. Then each category is thoroughly checked to spot inconsistencies, listings that may not be entirely reflective of actual market dealings, and lines too vague to be of merit. Only the best of the lot remains for publication. You'll find Schroeder's Antiques Price Guide the one to buy for factual information and quality.

No dealer, collector or investor can afford not to own this book. It is available from your favorite bookseller or antiques dealer at the low price of $12.95. If you are unable to find this price guide in your area, it's available from Collector Books, P.O. Box 3009, Paducah, KY 42002-3009 at $12.95 plus $2.00 for postage and handling.

8½ x 11", 608 Pages $12.95

COLLECTOR BOOKS

A Division of Schroeder Publishing Co., Inc.